All about Anne

Menno Metselaar and Piet van Ledden
Anne Frank's life story, with answers to frequently
asked questions and beautiful drawings
by Huck Scarry.

Anne with her friends on her
tenth birthday, 12 June 1939.

Z 1 Merwedeplein

Amsterdam-Z

Merwede Square

The Frank family lived in one of the new apartments on the Merwede Square in Amsterdam. This square also had the highest building in Amsterdam at that time. This building, which everyone called the Skyscraper, had twelve floors.

Leaving Germany

Otto and Edith Frank left Germany in 1933. After the summer of 1939, none of their family members lived there anymore. They fled Germany because of anti-Semitism from the Nazis, or had already left because of the poor economic situation.

12 June 1939

ESTONIA
LATVIA
SWEDEN
LITHUANIA
DENMARK
UNITED KINGDOM
THE NETHERLANDS
Amsterdam
London
Berlin
BELGIUM
Aachen
POLAND
SOVIET UNION
GERMANY
LUX.
Paris
Frankfurt-am-Main
FRANCE
SLOVAKIA
Basel
HUNGARY
SWITZERLAND
ROMANIA
YUGOSLAVIA
SPAIN
ITALY
BULGARIA
ALBANIA
TURKEY

"Happy birthday to you …"

It was Anne Frank's birthday! She was now ten years old and allowed to invite eight friends over. The girls posed happily for the photograph: Lucie van Dijk, Anne, Sanne Ledermann, Hannah Goslar, Juultje Ketellapper, Kitty Egyedi, Mary Bos, Ietje Swillens and Martha van den Berg. It was 12 June 1939, a sunny day in Amsterdam.

Sanne and Hannah were Anne's best friends. They had known each other since they were toddlers. Whenever the three of them were out on the street, people would say: "Look, there are Anne, Hanne and Sanne." Hannah and Sanne were from Berlin in Germany. Anne was also from Germany, but she was born in Frankfurt-am-Main.

Everyone got cake and lemonade and they brought presents for Anne. They played musical chairs and other games first, but because it was such a lovely day, they continued outside. Whoever won a game got a prize.

Anne's father, Otto Frank, took that Monday afternoon off work especially to be there with them. He took this photograph of Anne and her friends on the footpath in front of their house on Merwede Square.

Otto Frank had his own business. He sold a substance used in making jam called pectin. When the party was over, the girls were all given a pot of jam to take home. A few days later they were also given a print of the photograph to remember that lovely afternoon. Anne wrote on the back in her best handwriting: "Anne Frank's birthday party, 12-6-1939."

Nine little girls in a row. This was Anne's last birthday before World War II. Three of these girls would not survive the war because they were Jewish. Anne Frank was one of them. This is her story.

Chapter 1

A German girl

Anne Frank was born on a warm spring day. "Annelies Marie, born on 12 June 1929, 7.30 a.m.," her mother noted down in Anne's baby book. Anne was the second daughter of Otto Frank and Edith Frank-Holländer. Her sister Margot was three years older.

Two days later, Margot came to visit them in the hospital with grandmother Frank. "Margot is so delighted," Anne's mother wrote. Mother and baby were permitted to go home at the end of June. The Frank family lived on one floor of a large house in a leafy suburb of Frankfurt-am-Main. Grandmother Frank also lived in Frankfurt, but in the city center.

All of the neighborhood children were curious about the baby and came by to take a look at Anne. In early July, Edith's brothers Julius and Walter Holländer came to visit the new baby. A few weeks later Anne and her mother went to stay with grandmother Holländer, Edith's mother. She lived in Aachen, close to the Dutch border.

One neighbors' daughter in Frankfurt, Gertrud Naumann, was twelve years old and occasionally permitted to babysit. She played games with Margot and Anne and would read to them.

The Frank family also had a nanny: Kathi Stilgenbauer. Kathi noticed the two sisters were very different. Margot always looked like a little princess, while Anne could enjoy sitting on the balcony in a rain puddle. Kathi sometimes had to change Anne's clothes twice a day.

Margot, December 1927.

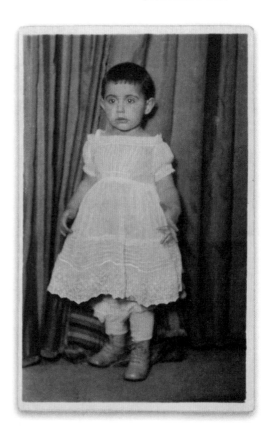

Newlyweds Otto and Edith Frank-Holländer with their wedding guests, 12 May 1925. Otto celebrated his 36th birthday on the same day.

Michael Frank
1851-1909

Alice Betty Stern
1865-1953

Helene Frank < > Erich Elias
1893-1986   1890-1984

Robert Frank < > Charlotte Witt
1886-1953   1900-1974

Herbert Frank
1891-1987

Otto Frank
1889-1980

Stephan Elias
1921-1980

Bernd Elias
1925-2015

Margot Betti Frank
1926-1945

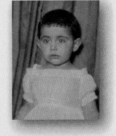

Annelies Marie Frank
1929-1945

Abraham Holländer
1860-1927

Rosa Stern
1866-1942

Edith Holländer
1900-1945

Julius Holländer
1894-1967

Walter Holländer
1897-1968

Bettina Holländer
1898-1914

When is someone Jewish?

Judaism is an ancient religion, just like Christianity and Islam. Many Jews also regard themselves as a member of the Jewish people. Most of them use the rule: You are Jewish if your mother is Jewish, it doesn't matter if you believe in it or not. So there are also Jews who are not religious. You can also become Jewish.

This means converting to Judaism. Just like with other religions, some people follow the rules of their faith very strictly, while others are little more flexible. Anne Frank was Jewish, because she had a Jewish mother. The Frank family did not live according to the stricter Jewish rules.

A synagogue in Frankfurt-Am-Main.
A synagogue is a Jewish place of worship.

Why did Hitler hate the Jews?

Adolf Hitler (1889-1945) was not the first to hate and target Jews, simply because of their religion, also known as anti-Semitism. For many centuries Jews were a small minority in many countries and were blamed for all kinds of problems. As a young man, Hitler lived in Vienna, Austria, where he heard many anti-Semitic ideas. He adopted these ideas. Hitler also felt that Austrians actually belonged to the German people. During World War I (1914-1918), Hitler fought in the German army as an Austrian. Germany lost this war. Hitler blamed the Jews for this defeat. This stirred up his anti-Semitic feelings even more.

Around 1920 Adolf Hitler became the leader of the NSDAP (the Nazi Party), just a small political party at the time. He wrote down his ideas for Germany in the book *Mein Kampf* (My Struggle). Hitler wanted to make Germany greater and more powerful than it had ever been before. He believed that people of the "Aryan race" were superior. The problems in Germany would be solved, Hitler believed, if all of the Jews were removed from the country. In this way he made the Jews into scapegoats.

Adolf Hitler at an SA meeting in Dortmund, October 1933.

"Our last hope: Hitler"

Bystanders looking at a poster at a Berlin crossroads in the winter of 1932. The election poster has just been attached to the column, because the stepladder is still there. The poster shows people looking back at the viewer in despair. The text reads: *Unsere letzte Hoffnung: Hitler* (Our last hope: Hitler) It's a poster for the Presidential election of March 1932. Hitler and his party said that they were going to solve Germany's problems. They generated propaganda (advertising) on the radio and at large mass meetings. Hitler was not elected President at this time, but a year later he was given the task of forming a government. In this way Hitler became the Chancellor (President) of Germany at the end of 1933.

While Anne's mother looked after the house and the children, Anne's father worked in his family's bank. The bank had been founded by Otto's father. The Frank family was German as well as Jewish and had a long history in Frankfurt: distant ancestors had lived there as long ago as the sixteenth century.

These were happy times. Otto and Edith were happy with their daughters. The family lived in a nice house and there were many children in the neighborhood to play with Margot and Anne. However, Anne's world was a world in crisis.

Germany had lost World War I (1914 - 1918). It had been agreed in the Peace Treaty of Versailles that Germany had to give up land to the victors and pay considerable reparations to other countries. Many Germans were bitter about this. They wanted to be out of this agreement.

To make matters worse, the New York stock exchange plummeted at the end of October 1929, causing a global economic crisis. Stocks were suddenly completely worthless. Many people lost all their money.

Germans were also hit hard by this. Millions of German citizens lost their jobs, had no more money and lived in poverty.

When things are going badly in any country, there are always people who blame others without any real justification. That also happened in Germany. Many Germans felt that the Jews were responsible for all of these problems, for losing the war and for the economic crisis.

There was also a political party that blamed the Jews for the crisis: the National Socialist German Labour Party (NSDAP). The leader of this party was Adolf Hitler, whose supporters were known as Nazis. They hated the Jews. The party program stated what they would change if they came into power. Jews would no longer be considered German and would only be permitted to stay in Germany as foreign visitors. They would not be permitted to work as public officials or teachers. And if there was not enough food for everyone, the Jews and all foreigners would be deported from the country. The NSDAP also wanted to close national borders and stop admitting people who were not German.

Anne, May 1931.

Otto with Margot and Anne, August 1931.

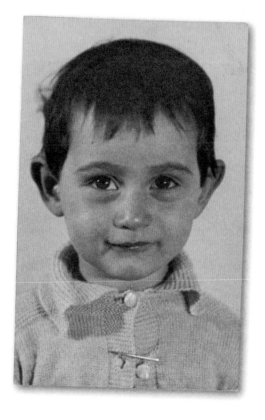

In 1929 the NSDAP was still small with few supporters, but three years later the party won the elections. One in three voters voted for Hitler's party. The Nazis promised Germany a golden future in which the country would be great and powerful. Adolf Hitler became the leader of the German government at the end of January 1933.

The NSDAP had a kind of private army: the SA (*Sturmabteilung*, or Storm Detachment). SA members wore a brown uniform, and would march through the streets and sing battle songs indicating they hated Jews. There were many fierce street fights between SA members and their political opponents, the communists and the social democrats.

Hitler and the NSDAP gradually turned Germany into a dictatorship. The Nazis threw thousands of political opponents in jail or imprisoned them in a concentration camp, such as the one at Dachau. Hundreds of them were murdered there.

The first swastika flags—the flags of the NSDAP—appeared in March 1933 on Frankfurt-am-Main city hall. On 1 April, throughout Germany SA members went into banks, shops, department stores and law offices owned by Jews, and Jewish doctors' surgeries. They tried to prevent customers there from entering these businesses. They carried cardboard signs which said: "German citizens! Resist! Do not buy from Jews."

Hitler's supporters did not stop at this. That May, they burned thousands of books written by Jews and other writers whom they felt were "Un-German" in Frankfurt and other German cities. These authors were no longer welcome in Nazi Germany and freedom of expression no longer existed. From that summer on, all other political parties were banned and there was only one party left: the NSDAP.

Otto and Edith wanted to leave. They felt threatened by Hitler and his supporters. Because of the economic crisis, the bank owned by the Frank family was not doing well either. With help from his brother-in-law Erich Elias, Otto was able to start a business in the Netherlands. He would sell Opekta (pectin), a substance used in making jam. Otto departed for

Margot and Anne in Aachen, October 1933.

A photograph of Edith, Anne and Margot from the machine in the Tietz department store, 10 March 1933. Together they weighed 110 kg.

Nazis hanging the swastika flag on the Frankfurt-Am-Main city hall, 13 March 1933.

Why w
the syr

The swas
symbol th
in India, f
this symb
and displa
posters, u
decoration
Struggle) i
represente
race." The
white and
German na
tween the
groups of p

Prisoners in Dachau concentration camp, 27 May 1933.

camp?

ower in 1933,
uilt in the
hau. This was
d their political
ncentration
, many people
persecution of

Jews and World War II. Hundreds of small and large concentration camps were built in Nazi Germany, and later in the occupied countries. People whom the Nazis felt were "undesirable," such as Jews, Roma, Sinti (gypsies), homosexuals and political opponents were imprisoned there without trial. The prisoners were forced to live in basic buildings (barracks) with wooden

bunk beds on a large area surrounded with barb wire and watch towers. They were forced to do very heavy labor and did not get much to eat or drink. The hygiene conditions were also very poor.

Amsterdam in the summer of 1933 and started out with a small office in the center of the city. He knew Amsterdam a little bit, because a branch of his family's bank had been set up there in 1924.

Edith, Margot and Anne remained in Germany a little longer. At the end of September they went to stay with grandmother Holländer in Aachen. Edith traveled regularly from Aachen to Amsterdam to look for a house. In November she found a suitable house on Merwede Square, in a newly built suburb in Amsterdam-Zuid. The house was smaller than the one in Frankfurt, but bright and warm.

Uncles Julius and Walter brought Margot to Amsterdam shortly before Christmas. She started at her new school there on 4 January 1934. Anne wanted to go with her sister, but had to stay with her grandmother a little longer. She was brought to Amsterdam in mid-February. Anne's life in a new country could finally begin.

Otto Frank's company dealt in pectin, a gel substance used in the making of jam. The business was housed at 263 Prinsengracht from December 1940.

Advertising poster for Opekta.

Chapter 2

A new country

Just like Margot, Anne wanted to start school right away, but she was still too young. In April 1934 she was finally allowed to go to kindergarten. Otto and Edith sent her to a Montessori school, where pupils were given plenty of freedom. They felt that this would be good for Anne.

More Jewish families who had left Nazi Germany lived around Merwede Square. Otto and Edith became friends with the Goslar family and the Ledermanns from Berlin. Hans Goslar and Franz Ledermann provided advice to Jews who wished to leave Nazi Germany, sell their business or wanted to start a new business someplace else. Anne, Hannah Goslar and Sanne Ledermann became friends. Hannah was with Anne at kindergarten, Sanne was in the same school as Margot.

Otto had to work hard to get his company going. Edith took care of the children and the housework and, just like in Frankfurt, the family had a maid. Edith kept in touch with their former neighbor Gertrud Naumann in Frankfurt. She wrote that Otto would not take any rest and that he was looking thin and tired. She also said in her letters that Margot and Anne talked about Gertrud often and missed her very much.

Anne turned five in June. The celebrations of her first birthday in the Netherlands started in Kindergarten and then continued with her friends at home. During the summer holidays Margot and Anne were permitted to go to a special holiday house for children in Zandvoort for two weeks. This was where they saw the sea for the first time! After the holiday, Margot went to third class, and Anne stayed in kindergarten for another year.

Anne, 11 September 1934.
Margot, 11 September 1934.

Margot and Anne in Zandvoort-aan-Zee, Summer 1934.

Anne with her friends Eva Goldberg (left) and Sanne Ledermann (center) on Merwede Square, August 1936.

"She ran into my arms."

"I was four years old when we went to live in Amsterdam. I saw Anne Frank that very first week in the grocery shop. My mother brought me to the kindergarten a few days later. I didn't want to stay there, because I didn't know anyone and didn't speak the language. But then I saw Anne ... She was making music with small metal chimes and when she finished, she turned around and ran into my arms. That's how we became friends. And our parents became friends too."

<u>Hannah Goslar</u>
Source: *Anne Frank Krant,*
Anne Frank House, 2015.

Anne and Hannah at the kindergarten, June 1935.

Forbidden love

Accompanied by the SA (*Sturmabteilung*, the paramilitary wing of the Nazi party), the Jew Julius Wolff and his gentile fiancée, Christine Neemann, were forced to walk the streets of the German city of Norden. It was Monday, 22 July 1935. Hundreds of people watched. Christine and Julius were both wearing a sign. Julian's sign said "I am a race desecrater," while Christine's said "I am a German girl and have allowed a Jew to desecrate me." The Nazis did not want Jews to be in relationships with people who were not Jewish. Christine and Julius were abused by the Nazis and thrown into prison. Christine was sent to a concentration camp. If she promised to end her relationship with Julius she would be released. Julius Wolff was imprisoned in another concentration camp. After some time he was released and managed to flee to the United States. This photograph was taken by the chemist of Norden, who was a member of the NSDAP and the SA. He took several photographs and displayed them in his shop window. The photographs were also published in a newspaper. What happened in Norden also took place in several other German cities. From September 1935, love relationships and marriages between Jews and non-Jews were legally prohibited in Nazi Germany.

By that time, Margot and Anne both spoke Dutch very well.

For Otto and Edith Frank, it was a relief to be out of Nazi Germany. They worried about family members who still lived there: Edith's mother and her brothers Julius and Walter. All of Otto's family members had already left: his brother Robert had moved to London, his brother Herbert lived in Paris and his sister Leni lived in Basel (Switzerland) with her husband Erich Elias and their sons Stephan and Bernd. Grandmother Frank had also lived there since 1933.

The situation in Nazi Germany became increasingly difficult for Jews. Jewish civil servants and teachers were fired from their jobs. Everywhere were signs with the text "Prohibited for Jews," at parks and swimming pools, for example. At access roads to cities and villages signs or large banners were put up with messages like "Jews are not welcome here" or "Jews are not wanted here." Using the newspapers and radio, the Nazis kept pumping out the message that Jews were "the misery of Germany." More and more Germans began to believe this hateful propaganda.

In September 1935, the Nazis went another step further. First, all citizens were required to state how many Jewish grandparents they had. Anyone with three of four Jewish grandparents was considered "fully Jewish," anyone with two Jewish grandparents was someone who the Nazis described as "half-Jewish," and those with one Jewish grandparent were "quarter-Jewish." Then the Nazis adopted special laws. Jews and non-Jews were not allowed to have love relationships and were thus not permitted to marry. German Jews were discriminated against more and more.

The Frank family was no longer able to visit their close relatives in Germany or Switzerland as often. It became more and more dangerous to travel through Nazi Germany. So naturally Anne was very excited when she was allowed to accompany her father to the family in Basel at the end of 1937. She had a lot of fun with her cousin Bernd. He was an enthusiastic figure skater and Anne decided she would also learn how to skate. In early 1938, Margot and Anne went to stay with grandmother Holländer in Aachen for the last time.

At the office, 1936. From left to right: Miep Santrouschitz (married Jan Gies in July 1941), Otto Frank and Henk van Beusekom.

The Ledermann family on their balcony, 1936. From left to right: Sanne, Ilse Ledermann-Citroen, Franz Ledermann and Barbara.

From left to right: Hannah Goslar, Anne, Dolly Citroen, Hannah Toby, Barbara Ledermann and Sanne Ledermann (standing). The photograph was taken in the Toby family's garden at Merwede Square, 1937.

Otto and Edith were having financial problems. The Opekta Company was not running as well as they had hoped, and the threat from Nazi Germany was becoming ever more serious. Otto traveled to Britain a few times to see if he could start a business there, but that did not work out. Then he met Hermann van Pels, who had also fled Nazi Germany with his family. Hermann knew everything about herbs and spices. With his business partner Johannes Kleiman, Otto Frank decided to start up a second company—Pectacon—which would concentrate on the grinding, mixing and selling of herbs and spices. They employed Hermann van Pels.

In Nazi Germany, the situation became even grimmer. During the night of 9 to 10 November 1938, the Nazis set hundreds of synagogues on fire and destroyed thousands of shops owned by Jews. More than one hundred Jews were murdered and as many as 30,000 Jewish men were arrested. Julius and Walter Holländer, Edith's brothers and Anne and Margot's uncles, were among them. Julius was released, because he had fought for Germany in World War I. Walter, however, was sent to Sachsenhausen concentration camp. This night went down in history as the *Kristallnacht* the "Night of Broken Glass," because of the broken window panes that lay everywhere on the streets.

Julius and Otto tried to get Walter released. They achieved this in early December. Walter was given permission by the Dutch Aliens Service to come to the Netherlands and he was released. Walter ended up in a refugee camp in Amsterdam. He was not allowed to work, and was obliged to pay for his accommodation. Refugees were under police supervision and not allowed to leave the camp without permission.

Grandmother Holländer came to Amsterdam in March 1939. She moved in with the Frank family. Julius managed to emigrate to the United States via Amsterdam in April. Walter was able to follow him in December. They had to leave all of their possessions behind in Aachen, had been forced to give up their business in metals and would have to start all over again in America. They went to live in the vicinity of Boston. Walter found simple work in a cardboard factory; Julius in a leather factory.

Anne with her father during a boat trip, 1938.

A class photo of Anne from the Montessori school, 1938.

A great and powerful Germany

A German military parade in Nuremberg, September 1935. After World War I, Germany was required to relinquish land to the victors. This was agreed in the Peace Treaty of Versailles, because Germany started the war. Not only did Hitler and the Nazis want that land back, they also wanted more land with it. In 1938, Hitler was able to add Austria and parts of Czechoslovakia to Nazi Germany without any conflict. Britain and France allowed this to happen. After World War I, which had created millions of casualties, they did not want another war in Europe. But the Nazis felt that the German people needed more *Lebensraum* (space to live in), and saw opportunities for this in Eastern Europe. This was why Nazi Germany built up a large, modern army.

The attack on Poland

German soldiers marching through a Polish village. The German army invaded Poland on 1 September 1939. The Polish army was not equipped to fight the Germans, who had many modern weapons. Nazi Germany and the Soviet Union had secretly agreed to divide Poland between them: the western part was for Nazi Germany, the east was for Russia. The German front soldiers were followed by special army units of the SS. These SS members shot dead more than 60,000 Polish citizens in four months, among them 7,000 Jews. The Nazis imprisoned the Polish Jews in ghettoes, which were closed-off sections in a town or city. Later, Jewish men, women and children were transported to the concentration and extermination camps from these ghettoes.

Anne celebrated her tenth birthday on 12 June. She had been living in the Netherlands for six years and was in fourth class of the Montessori school. After the summer holiday Anne went into the fifth class (group 7), while Margot went into the second year of the Girls' Lyceum (grammar school).

The German army invaded Poland on 1 September 1939. France and Britain had promised to support Poland if the country were to be attacked. They declared war on Nazi Germany but did not send any soldiers to Poland. Tensions increased when Nazi Germany also invaded Denmark and Norway in April 1940.

The Frank family followed the news on these war developments very closely. At the end of April 1940, Margot wrote to her American pen pal Betty Ann Wagner: "We listen to the radio a lot because it's a tense time. Because we share a border with Germany and we are a small country, we never feel safe."

A little verse from Anne in the friendship album of her friend Juultje Ketellapper.

Grandmother Holländer's passport

Chapter 3

War!

In the night of 9 to 10 May 1940, the Frank family was woken by the sounds of heavy explosions and aircraft. From their house they could see Schiphol Airport being bombed. The very thing they had feared the most was happening: the Netherlands was under attack by the German army. It was war!

In Amsterdam, panic broke out among Jewish residents. In particular those who had fled Germany after *Kristallnacht* knew all too well what the Nazis were capable of. They had seen it from up close. Some drove to IJmuiden harbor and tried to get to Britain by boat. Very few succeeded. Others were so desperate that they committed suicide. They did not want to wait for the Nazis to come for them.

After a few days it became clear that the Dutch army was going to lose. The German army had modern weapons and was well trained. Queen Wilhelmina and her government fled to Britain. When German planes bombed the center of Rotterdam on 14 May, Dutch military leaders conceded. The Netherlands was occupied: the Nazis were now in control.

After the German invasion, life went on as usual for the Frank family. Anne and Margot could go to school from 20 May, and nothing much seemed to have changed. However, Anne's birthday on 12 June was not celebrated, because nobody was in the mood for it. They went to the beach a few times during the summer holidays. Then Anne started her last year at the primary school.

Anne, May 1940.

Anne with Miss Godron and her classmates Martha van den Berg (left) and Rela Salomon (right), 1940.

Mei 1940

Mei 1940

Margot, May 1940.

Why did Hitler attack the Netherlands?

The Nazi Germany attack on the Netherlands in May 1940 was part of a huge plan of attack to defeat France. Just like it was in World War I, the Netherlands was neutral. The Netherlands did not choose to support Germany, but did not wish to support Britain and France either. Hitler did not care that the Netherlands was neutral. According to German army leaders, in order to be able to defeat France, the Netherlands, Belgium and Luxembourg had to be conquered. In this way, the German army could avoid the strong French line of defence at the border between Germany and France. Once France was conquered, Hitler's plan was to launch an attack on Britain from the ports of Belgium and the Netherlands.

German soldiers with a dead Dutch soldier, May 1940. That May approximately 2,200 Dutch soldiers were killed.

How did the Nazis know who was Jewish?

In January 1941, all Jews were obliged to register with the authorities in the Netherlands. The Nazis had already established in race laws who they considered to be Jewish: anyone with at least one Jewish grandparent was obliged to buy a form from the municipal council and complete it. 160,000 Jews lived in the Netherlands. As many as 15,000 of these had previously escaped from Nazi Germany. This registration was organized by Dutch civil servants. In this way, the German occupier knew exactly who was Jewish in the spring of 1941. A large black "J" was stamped in two places on the identity documents of Jews.

?

BEWIJS VAN AANMELDING,

als bedoeld in artikel 9, eerste lid, van de Verordening No. 6/1941 van den Rijks-commissaris voor het bezette Nederlandsche gebied, betreffende den aanmeldingsplicht van personen van geheel of gedeeltelijk joodschen bloede.

JOODSCHE RAAD VOOR AMSTERDAM

✳

De ondergeteekende, ambtenaar voor de aanmelding, verklaart dat de aan keerzijde aangeduide persoon, opgenomen in het Bevolkingsregister dezer gemeente, heeft voldaan aan de verplichting tot aanmelding volgens de bovengenoemde Verordening.

Afgegeven op __20 MAART 1941__

in Gemeente __AMSTERDAM__

voor den Burgemeester,
De Administrateur
afd. Bev.register en Verkiezingen.

Every Jewish resident was given this card as proof of registration. Personal details were on the back.

Dutch Nazis

Dutch Nazis greeting German soldiers with the Hitler salute on 16 May 1940. They are standing on the Berlagebrug in Amsterdam. In the Netherlands, a political party that agreed with Hitler and the Nazis was set up in 1931: the Nationalist Socialist Movement, or NSB. The party was led by Anton Mussert. In 1935, the NSB gained almost 8 percent of votes in the election. In 1943, the NSB had a record number of members, as many as 100,000. Because they were collaborating with the German occupier, many Dutch people hated NSB supporters. Just like the NSDAP, the NSB had a youth organisation, the *Jeugdstorm*, and a type of private army, the *Weerafdeling* (WA).

The February strike

During the winter of 1940-1941, the general mood in the occupied Netherlands became even grimmer. Dutch Nazis attacked Jews and destroyed their belongings. Fights broke out between *Weerafdeling* members and Jews on the streets and in cafés. A WA man was seriously injured in one Amsterdam fight and died later. Things remained unsettled. In revenge, the German occupiers carried out *razzias*. More than 400 Jewish men were captured and transported to the Mauthausen concentration camp. Many Dutch people were extremely shocked by this. On 25 February 1941, thousands of people in Amsterdam and the surrounding areas stopped work and went on strike in protest against the persecution of the Jews. The Nazis were surprised. After two days, the strikes were brought down very harshly: nine strikers were shot dead, 24 people were injured and dozens were arrested. The strike in February was the only mass protest against the persecution of Jews in occupied Europe.

A German soldier guarding Jewish prisoners, 22 February 1941.

The Nazis also started to exclude Jews in the Netherlands, as they had already done in Germany. They implemented anti-Semitic measures: Jewish civil servants and public officials were fired from their jobs, Jews were no longer permitted membership in the air protection squad and the slaughtering of animals according to Jewish religious laws was forbidden.

These first measures did not really affect Anne and her family. However, in October, all Jewish business owners were required to register with the occupying forces. Otto knew that this was the first step: his businesses would be taken from him. In Nazi Germany, Jews were no longer permitted to own businesses.

Otto Frank came up with a solution. He asked his employees Johannes Kleiman and Victor Kugler and Jan Gies, Miep's husband, to take over the management of Opekta and Pectacon. They would formally become the new directors, but they would naturally discuss all important issues with Otto Frank.

That winter, Anne had a new passion: figure skating. She wrote enthusiastically to her cousins in Switzerland that she had been given new skates and was taking lessons. "I'm on the ice rink every free minute I have. (...) I'm now taking regular figure skating classes, I'm learning to waltz, jump, and everything to do with figure skating." Anne hoped to be as good a figure skater as her cousin Bernd, who was already performing in public.

Otto and Edith were worried about the anti-Semitic measures, but they tried to hide this from Margot and Anne. In January 1941 all Jews with at least one Jewish grandparent were required to register with the city council. They had to enter the following details on all forms: their name, address, age, place of birth, nationality, civil status (for example married or divorced) and profession, as well as their religion, how many Jewish grandparents they had and, if applicable, their last place of residence in Germany. Now the Nazis knew exactly where Jews lived.

By February, the atmosphere in Amsterdam was menacing. The first large razzia took place in the city center. German police

Anne (second from left) in the Vondelpark in Amsterdam, winter 1940-1941. She loved figure skating. This is the only photograph of Anne skating that has survived.

Johannes Kleiman (left) with Victor Kugler in front of the door of 263 Prinsengracht, in the early nineteen fifties.

arrested hundreds of Jewish men and took them away to the Mauthausen concentration camp. Over the following year, many families would receive notification that their husbands or sons who had been taken away had died.

Otto and Edith feared the worst. They called on an old college friend of Otto's named Nathan Straus for help. He lived in the United States. Otto and Edith wanted to escape the occupied Netherlands to America. Uncles Julius and Walter were also asked to help with this. But America would only accept a small number of refugees. In addition, they needed visas and permission to leave the Netherlands. Arranging these things would take a lot of time and money.

There was another razzia in June, this time in the district where the Frank family lived. Around 300 Jewish men were arrested and taken away, including friends and acquaintances of the Frank family. This took place on 11 June, the day before Anne's birthday. The birthday party was postponed because of the razzia and because grandmother Holländer was seriously ill.

During that summer holiday, Anne was allowed to stay with her friend Sanne Ledermann for two weeks. Sanne's parents had rented a holiday home in Beekbergen, near Apeldoorn. Anne learned how to play table tennis and read a lot, because the weather was frequently bad. Sanne and Anne would occasionally look after baby Ray, whose parents were acquaintances and who also stayed there. Anne wrote in a letter to her grandmother Frank that she slept a lot better in Beekbergen. She was not disturbed by air-raid alarms or the sound of anti-aircraft guns.

In August, Otto and Edith received a letter from the Amsterdam Municipal Council. The Nazis had adopted a new rule: all Jewish schoolchildren were required to attend separate schools after the summer holiday. Margot and Anne had to say good-bye to their classmates and their teachers.

There were already Jewish schools in Amsterdam, as well as Roman Catholic and Protestant ones. But in order to be able to suddenly accommodate almost 7,000 Jewish schoolchildren, new schools had to be set up. The Jewish Lyceum was one of

Anne and Sanne Ledermann on holiday in Beekbergen with Ray, the baby of acquaintances of the Ledermann family.

The Frank family on Merwede Square, 1941.

14

"We don't do much at school …"

Anne Frank made this drawing. She wrote her name on it, and it was probably the teacher who wrote down the date: 20 June 1941. Anne wrote a long letter to her grandmother Frank in Switzerland: "We don't do much at school, in the mornings we draw a little and in the afternoons we sit in the garden catching flies and picking flowers." Anne's school had a large garden which the children maintained themselves.

More than a hundred anti-Jewish measures

The Nazis created more and more ways to exclude Jews from society, also in the Netherlands. More than a hundred anti-Semitic measures were implemented during the first years of the occupation. Some examples of these are listed below:

- All Jewish civil servants were fired.
- Jews were forbidden to have their own businesses.
- Jews were no longer allowed to visit non-Jewish households and vice versa.
- Jews were allowed to possess a maximum of 110 guilders (about € 775 in today's money). They had to hand in the rest of their money to the authorities.
- Jews were forbidden membership in (sports) organizations where there were non-Jewish members.
- Jews were only allowed to buy groceries in the afternoons between three and five o'clock.
- Public transport and public amenities, such as swimming pools and parks, were prohibited for Jews.
- Jewish schoolchildren had to go to separate Jewish schools.
- Jews were required to get permission to travel or move house.
- All Jews age six or older were required to wear a Star of David.

Voor Joden verboden

DE PROCUREUR-GENERAAL
FUNG. GEWESTELIJK DIRECTEUR VAN POLITIE

VAN GENECHTEN

From September 1941, signs with "Jews Prohibited" or "Jews Not Wanted" were hung in many places in the Netherlands, by law.

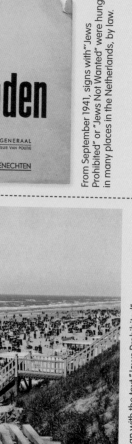

A sign with the text "Jews Prohibited" on the beach at Zandvoort, spring 1941.

Fighting for Nazi Germany

In August 1941, a train full of Dutch men left the station in The Hague for the east. They had voluntarily signed up to fight with the German army against the Russians. Nazi Germany had launched its attack on the Soviet Union (Russia) and could make good use of these Dutch volunteers. Family and friends gave them an enthusiastic send-off, with the Hitler salute.

Many short texts were chalked onto the train: "To where the Jews are" (compared to the Netherlands, many Jews lived in Russia at that time), "We're off to get Stalin" and a hangman's noose with the text "Stalin must hang from this" (Stalin was the Soviet leader). The V for victory and the swastika were also chalked onto the train. One of the men is proudly displaying his copy of *Mein Kampf* (My Struggle), the book written by Hitler. Every volunteer was given a copy of the book. As many as 25,000 went to fight with the German army, of whom 7,000 perished.

A truly global war

On 7 December 1941, Japanese aircrafts attacked the American naval base and ships at Pearl Harbor, Hawaii, in the Pacific Ocean. Like Germany in Europe, Japan wanted to have control over East Asia. Immediately after this attack, the United States declared war on Japan and its ally Nazi Germany. And thus the war in Europe became a World War, with the "Axis Powers" (Nazi Germany, Italy and Japan) on one side and the "Allied Forces" (the United States, Canada, Britain, France, Russia and China) on the other. As in Europe, there was heavy fighting in Asia, along with millions of victims. About a month after the attack on Pearl Harbor, on 11 January 1942, Japanese soldiers landed in the Dutch East Indies (now Indonesia). Japan occupied the Dutch colony, and white Dutch citizens were locked up in special districts, known as the "Japanese camps."

Burning ships of the American Navy at Pearl Harbor, December 7, 1941.

these new schools. Margot went into the fourth year, and Anne went into the first year, as did her friend Hannah. Everything still had to be arranged before the school could start. This was why the school year did not begin until 15 October.

In mid-September, Anne went on a trip with her father for a few days. Otto wanted a few days of peace and quiet. He took Anne with him to a nice hotel near Arnhem. She loved it there, in the middle of the countryside.

On the first day of school at the Jewish Lyceum, Anne and Hannah discovered they would not be in the same class. Anne did not know any of her new classmates. She felt very alone. The third lesson was gym and Anne liked the gym teacher so much that she dared to ask her for help. The teacher arranged for Hannah and Anne to be together in the same class from the next lesson on.

On 7 December 1941 Japanese aircraft bombed ships belonging to the American Navy at Pearl Harbor (Hawaii). This meant war between Japan and the United States. But because Japan and Nazi Germany were allies, Nazi Germany and the United States were at war now, too. Borders were closed. Any hope that Anne's parents had for getting out of the Netherlands were now gone. Escaping had now become almost impossible.

For the Frank family, 1942 had a sad beginning. Grandmother Holländer had already been ill for a long time, and died at the end of January. She was buried at the Jewish cemetery in Hoofddorp. Anne now had one grandparent left, her grandmother Frank, who lived in Basel.

Anne occasionally wrote to her grandmother and other family members in Switzerland. She could not write everything she wanted in these letters, as the post was being checked by the Nazis. In April 1942 Anne wrote that she was afraid that she had forgotten everything she had learned about figure skating, because she had not been able to do it for so long. What she did not say was that skating was actually forbidden to Jews.

Anne also wrote that she "liked" school at the Jewish Lyceum, but complained about the amount of homework she had to do and

Anne in Beekbergen, June 1941.
From left to right: Anne, Tineke Gatsonides, Sanne and Barbara Ledermann.

Margot (left) on a break with her fellow members of the Zionist youth organization *Maccabi Hatzair* during a cycling excursion, 1941.
Anne writes in her diary that Margot would like to become a nurse in Palestine.

because of this, had very little time for other things. There were more boys than girls in Anne's class. She wrote: "At the start we talked and played with the boys a lot but it has cooled off a bit, happily, because they've become really annoying."

Anne also mentioned Moortje, her black cat, in that letter. She hoped that there would soon be kittens. That could certainly have been the case: Moortje would often go out wandering and there were many tomcats in the neighborhood. According to Anne, Sanne also loved Moortje. Even though Sanne was at a different school, Anne still saw her regularly. Her friend Hannah had a little sister who Anne thought was "really cute" and could already walk. Anne hoped to receive a reply from Switzerland soon.

Anne's parents had given up their plans to flee. Johannes Kleiman came up with the idea to set up a hiding place and wait out the war in it. One section of Otto Frank's business premises—the annex at the back—was empty and that seemed to be a suitable place. Otto and Edith agreed to go into hiding there with Hermann van Pels and his family, as there was enough room

for two families. They hoped the Nazis would not find them.

Otto Frank, Hermann van Pels and Johannes Kleiman gradually set up the second and third floors of the annex. They had to be careful because no one was to notice these preparations. Hence furniture, groceries and other items belonging to the Frank family were moved to the hiding place via Johannes Kleiman's apartment. This took place in the evenings and over weekends.

Otto asked the other office employees in his company—Victor Kugler, Miep Gies and Bep Voskuijl—if they would also help if the family had to go into hiding. This meant making sure they would have everything they needed to live. Otto's employees promised to do this, despite knowing that the penalties for helping Jews were extremely harsh.

Anne turned thirteen on Friday 12 June 1942. She was given something she had wanted very badly and was allowed to choose herself: a diary. Anne was a little bit pampered this year, because she had not

Miep married Jan Gies on 16 July 1941.

Otto and Anne among other guests at Miep and Jan Gies' wedding, 16 July 1941.

16

"A tight group"

"After school we were together every day. I would help Anne with maths. (…) We would have a great time together, Anne and me. We enjoyed school and our lessons. The teachers were separated for the same reasons we were and we formed a tight group. When we were at school, we would temporarily forget that the Germans had occupied the country. The war was never mentioned in class and our parents told us as little as possible about what was going on around us."

Jacqueline van Maarsen
Source: Jacqueline van Maarsen, *Je beste vriendin Anne* (Your best friend Anne), Querido, 2011.

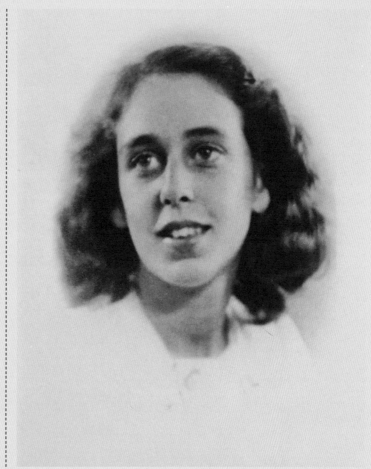

Jacqueline van Maarsen, around 1943.

A home cinema

Anne Frank loved films. She collected photographs of film stars. From September 1941, Jews were no longer permitted to enter cinemas. As a result, some Jews, including the Frank family, held film screenings at home. Anne and her friend Jacqueline made real tickets for these screenings. The row and chair number is on the ticket for the screening of Sunday 1 March 1942, which Jacqueline has kept. The ticket is even stamped.

Jacqueline.v.Maarsen. wordt uitgenodigd opZondag. 1. Maart bij Anne Frank,Merwedeplein 37,te 11 uur, voor een filmvoorstelling.

&&& ___ &&& ___ &&& ___ &&& ___

MRT 1942

Z.O.Z.

Zonder deze kaart geen toegang.

——————-

Wanneer men verhinderd is te komen, gelieve tijdig te waarschuwen.

MRT 1942

tel.90441

rij II plaats2

Why didn't the Jews simply take off the Star of David?

The Nazis implemented the Star of David in Germany and in most of the occupied countries in Europe. All Jews in the Netherlands older than six years were required to wear the star from 3 May 1942. They even had to buy those stars themselves, maximum four per person. Jews who were inspected on the street and were not wearing a star could be imprisoned for six months or be given a hefty fine of 1000 guilders (€6500 in today's money). The German and Dutch police could easily check if someone was Jewish, because from May 1941 all Jews in the Netherlands had a letter "J" on their personal identity documents. In practice, Jews not wearing the star were arrested by the Nazis and immediately sent to Camp Westerbork.

Anne's diary

Anne was given this diary on her thirteenth birthday, on 12 June 1942. She was allowed to pick one out in a neighborhood bookshop. When Anne was in hiding in the Secret Annex, the diary became very important to her. On 16 March 1944, she wrote: "the best thing of all is that at least I can still write down what I think and feel, otherwise I would suffocate."

been able to really celebrate her eleventh and twelfth birthdays properly. She was given sweets, books, flowers, a game and naturally special birthday cards from Switzerland.

At school, Anne shared butter cookies with everyone and at gym she was allowed to choose the game. She chose volleyball. Unfortunately, she herself could not play because her arm was prone to dislocating at the shoulder. Anne invited her girlfriends back to her house after school to celebrate her birthday.

Helmut Silberberg gave Anne six lovely carnations. Helmut—who everyone called Hello—was not in Anne's school. She knew him through a girl from the neighborhood. Hello was already sixteen and, like Anne, came from Germany. Anne liked him. They would often go to Delphi and Oasis, two ice-cream parlors in the neighborhood. Jews were allowed to go to these as they were Jewish businesses. Many other places had "Prohibited to Jews" signs outside them.

Anne's real birthday party was on Sunday. She invited the entire class from the Jewish Lyceum. Jewish children were no longer allowed into cinemas, so Anne's father showed an exciting film at home: *Rin Tin Tin - Lighthouse by the Sea*. Otto Frank then showed a film he himself was very proud of: an advertising film for Opekta.

After her birthday, Anne started to write in her diary with great enthusiasm. She briefly told her life story and described her classmates in a few sentences. She did not hold back. She really could not stand some of her classmates.

At school, the conversations were mainly about the reports. Who would go on to the next class? Who would stay behind? Some boys would even take bets on it. Finally, on Friday 3 July, the day of reckoning arrived. All of the schoolchildren and teachers gathered in the Jewish concert hall. After music and serious speeches, the children got their reports. Anne was not dissatisfied. Algebra was the only subject in which she did poorly, otherwise she got two sixes (satisfactory), seven sevens (more than satisfactory) and two eights (good). The summer holidays could begin.

A school photo of Anne from the Jewish Lyceum, December 1941.

A school photo of Margot from the Jewish Lyceum, December 1941.

Hello called to see Anne on Sunday morning. It was nice and warm and they sat on the balcony chatting. When Hello was leaving he promised to come back that afternoon. The doorbell rang again around three o'clock. Anne was reading on the balcony.

Anne's mother opened the door and got a huge fright. It was a police officer! He handed her a card, which stated that Margot had to register with the police. As soon as he was gone, Edith immediately went to Hermann van Pels. Otto was not at home at that time, he was out visiting with an acquaintance from Frankfurt.

Margot told Anne that their father had been called up to register to work for the Nazis in Germany. When Edith returned with Hermann van Pels, the front door was locked and nobody was allowed to open it.

When Anne later learned that the message was not for her father, but for Margot, she burst into tears. Did Margot really have to go to a horrible work camp? Alone? She was just sixteen years old! Edith calmed Anne down; they were well prepared and would

leave together the next day. Then the doorbell rang again! Anne thought it might be Hello, but the front door had to stay closed. When the telephone rang shortly after, she was allowed to answer it. It was her friend Jacqueline van Maarsen. They chatted for a bit, but Anne could tell her nothing about Margot's message.

Anne's father returned home at five that afternoon. When he heard the news, he immediately telephoned Johannes Kleiman and asked him to come over. Hermann van Pels went to Miep and Jan Gies to ask if they would also help. Otto and Edith wanted to give them as many items as they could for the hiding place. The helpers came and went to the Frank family's house until late that night. Margot and Anne also gathered their things. Anne stuffed everything into her schoolbag: her diary was the first thing, but also old letters, school books, hair curlers, handkerchiefs, a comb ...

It was half-past eleven by the time Anne went to bed. Where could this mysterious hiding place be? Exhausted, she fell fast asleep in her own bed for the last time.

Otto Frank showed the film *Rin Tin Tin - Lighthouse by the Sea* at home during Anne's thirteenth birthday party. They could not watch the film about the adventures of the dog Rin Tin Tin in the cinema because cinemas were "Prohibited for Jews."

A secret meeting

On 20 January 1942, fifteen high-ranking Nazis gathered in a villa at Lake Wannsee near Berlin. It was a secret meeting in which the Nazis discussed how they could eradicate the Jews from Europe, on Hitler's orders. It was agreed that the Jews would be transported by train to concentration and extermination camps in Eastern Europe. There they would die of forced heavy labor or be exterminated. The report of this meeting has been preserved. The list indicates per country how many Jews lived there. In total there were eleven million Jews in Europe, of whom as many as 160,000 lived in the Netherlands.

Land	Zahl
A. Altreich	131.800
Ostmark	43.700
Ostgebiete	420.000
Generalgouvernement	2.284.000
Bialystok	400.000
Protektorat Böhmen und Mähren	74.200
Estland - judenfrei -	
Lettland	3.500
Litauen	34.000
Belgien	43.000
Dänemark	5.600
Frankreich / Besetztes Gebiet	165.000
Unbesetztes Gebiet	700.000
Griechenland	69.600
Niederlande	160.800
Norwegen	1.300
B. Bulgarien	48.000
England	330.000
Finnland	2.300
Irland	4.000
Italien einschl. Sardinien	58.000
Albanien	200
Kroatien	40.000
Portugal	3.000
Rumänien einschl. Bessarabien	342.000
Schweden	8.000
Schweiz	18.000
Serbien	10.000
Slowakei	88.000
Spanien	6.000
Türkei (europ. Teil)	55.500
Ungarn	742.800
UdSSR	5.000.000
Ukraine 2.994.684	
Weißrußland aus- schl. Bialystok 446.484	
Zusammen: über	11.000.000

K210405   372029

"I was really disappointed"

On Sunday afternoon 5 July 1942, Hello Silberberg rang the Frank family's doorbell. He had arranged with Anne that he would come visit, but nobody opened the door to him. Hello talked about this in an interview after the war: **"I was really disappointed and wondered what had happened. The next day I rang the doorbell again a few times, but the door remained closed."**

Hello Silberberg
Source: *Anne Frank Magazine*,
Anne Frank House, 1998.

A passport photograph of Hello (Helmut) Silberberg, 1942.

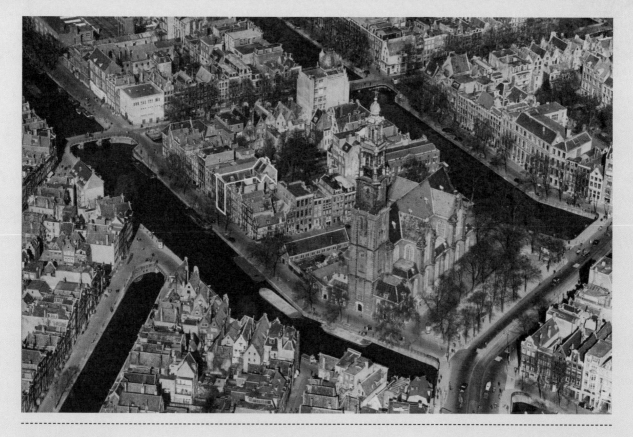

Prinsengracht 263

This aerial photograph from 1949 shows the front of the house and the Secret Annex at 263 Prinsengracht. This was the building which housed Otto Frank's business.

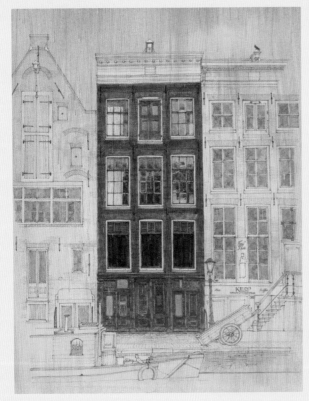

The front / The back

The front of Otto Frank's business. On the left was a cabinet-maker's, on the right a tea and food shop.

The back of Otto Frank's business. Sometimes Anne would look out from the attic window in the Secret Annex to the chestnut tree and the birds in the sky.

Chapter 4

In hiding

The next morning Anne's mother woke her up at half-past five. She had to put on as many of her clothes as possible. They could not walk along the streets with suitcases, people would notice. Anne pulled on as many items as she could: two shirts, two pairs of trousers, a skirt and a dress. She was very warm, it was a humid day and raining outside.

Anne had to leave her cat Moortje behind: she could not come. Anne left a letter to the neighbors asking them to take care of the cat. Anne's mother Edith also left a piece of paper with an address in Maastricht. The Frank family were hoping that this would trick people into thinking that they had fled to Switzerland via Maastricht.

Miep Gies came to fetch Margot at half-past seven. Margot had removed the yellow Star of David from her jacket and left with Miep on a bicycle. Otto, Edith and Anne followed on foot soon after. They had everything with them in bags. Now if they could manage not to get caught …

Anne did not learn where they were going until they were on their way. Their hiding place would be in her father's business! They arrived there after an hour of walking. Miep was waiting and opened the door for them. Soaking wet from rain and sweat, they went inside and climbed the small staircase to the Secret Annex. A nervous Margot was already waiting. Everyone was relieved they had not been stopped by street patrols on their way and happy that they had all arrived safely.

The Secret Annex itself was still a big mess, with boxes full of things, food supplies,

1942 – 1944

Just after half-past seven on Monday 6 July 1942, Anne and her parents went to the hiding place. Anne would never see Moortje again.

furniture, all strewn around. Otto and Edith did not plan to go into hiding until 16 July, but because Margot received her notification, their plans had changed. The first few days in the Secret Annex were taken up with tidying and organizing the place.

The neighbors could not be allowed to see them, so Otto and Anne immediately made curtains. These were not particularly nice, simply some sheets stitched together. Otto also took care of the blackout curtains. In the occupied Netherlands, windows had to be blacked out at night, no light could come out of the houses. The street lights were also off. This was to make it difficult for Allied bombers to find their way to German cities.

Anne did not have time to write in her diary for a few days. Her life changed completely from one day to the next. A week previously she had still been in school, she had met Hello and her friends in the afternoons and had been looking forward to the summer holidays. Now she was hidden inside her father's office building and no longer permitted to go outside. How long would she have to stay here?

The Van Pels family arrived at the Secret Annex on 13 July: Hermann, his wife Auguste and their son Peter. Anne already knew Peter. He had been to her thirteenth birthday and brought her some chocolate. He wasn't really her type, she found him boring and shy. Peter had brought his cat: Mouschi. Anne had to get used to Mouschi. She missed Moortje... Would the neighbors take good care of her?

Anne wrote a goodbye letter to her friend Jacqueline. They had promised to write to each other if either of them had to go away unexpectedly. But Anne's father would not let her send the letter: that was too dangerous. In her diary, Anne fantasized about receiving a reply from Jacqueline and wrote her another letter.

Anne read all the books she was able to bring from her favorite writer Cissy van Marxveldt. These books were about the experiences of Joop ter Heul and her friends. Anne started to write to the friends of Joop ter Heul in her diary: Marianne, Emmy, Pop, Phien, Conny, Lou, Kitty and Jet. She pretended they were her own friends. However, there were so many that

Miep Gies taking the steep staircase to the communal living room and kitchen in the Secret Annex. Peter's cat Mouschi, watches her.

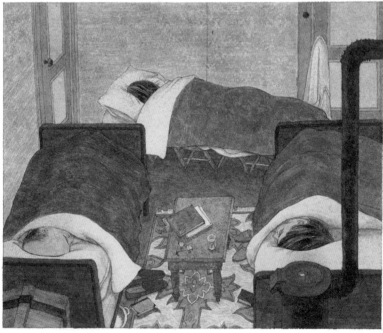

After the arrival of Fritz Pfeffer, Margot had to share a room with her parents.

1

2

3

Bookcase

In August 1942, Victor Kugler came up with the idea of covering the access door to the Secret Annex (1) with a moveable bookcase.

First one of the steps was removed, and a wooden partition was made for the uppermost part of the door (2). A map of Belgium was hung above the moveable bookcase. The shelves within the bookcase were organised in such a way that it looked exactly like the office archives (3).

Blacking out

The windows in the Secret Annex were screened off. By day, this was done with net curtains (2). Light could come inside, but nobody outside could see in. In the evenings the windows were blacked out using panels covered with dark cloth (3). Blacking out windows between sunset and sunrise was required by the German occupier. Because they could not see any lights of villages, towns or industrial areas, it was very difficult for crews of Allied bombers to determine where they were flying.

The tiny room shared by Anne Frank and Fritz Pfeffer in the nineteen fifties. The remains of the net curtain are still hanging.

2

3

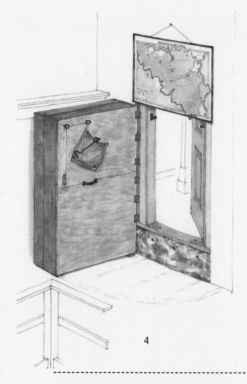

4

5

The bookcase, 1954.

The bookcase was made by Bep Voskuijl's father, who worked in the warehouse. Behind the moveable bookcase was a hook (4). The helpers and people in hiding could raise the hook and then push it open. The people in hiding had to get used to the new "door." They often banged their heads. After a few days Peter made a cushion so that they would not bang their heads so hard (5).

"I had to help them…"

"There was nothing else I could do. I had to help them: they were my friends. I told my wife nothing: she was very sick. I didn't want to alarm her, and so I couldn't talk about it at home. As for those in hiding, their lives changed completely. They had to stay really quiet, especially during the day. But for us, the helpers, it was also a tense and anxious time. Our greatest fear was that their hiding place would be discovered. I had to stage a good show for Otto Frank's former business associates, for customers and neighbors."

Victor Kugler
Source: *Anne Frank House.*
A museum with a story,
Anne Frank House, 1999.

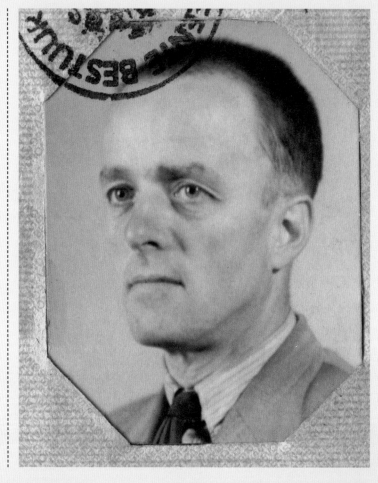

Victor Kugler, around 1944.

Anne eventually chose one: Kitty. This became the friend to whom Anne wrote in her diary.

Writing was the only way for Anne to get some release. All the adults around her sometimes drove her crazy, treating her like a small child. And she could never slam a door, stamp her feet or even just go outside.

Anne also described what was going on in the world outside in her diary. The reports from Amsterdam worsened. More and more Jews were being summoned to register with the authorities. If they did not, they would be dragged from their homes by the Nazis, usually at night. The Dutch police helped with this, the helpers told the group hiding in the Secret Annex. Bep Voskuijl also told Anne that her classmate Betty Bloemendal had been taken away. Anne was shocked and very worried: how would things go for her friends?

Another source of news for the people in hiding was the radio located downstairs in Otto's office. The first time they went down to listen to the news there, Anne was terrified. Imagine if the neighbors heard

anything! She wanted to get back up to the safety of the Secret Annex as quickly as possible. Later she became used to being able to go to other parts of the building in the evenings, at night and during the weekends. She even enjoyed these opportunities to leave the tiny and cramped hiding place for a little while.

In September, Miep Gies asked Otto Frank if there was room for another person to join the group: Fritz Pfeffer was a common acquaintance. The people in hiding and the helpers all decided that he could join them. Margot would move into her parents' bedroom and Fritz Pfeffer would sleep in Anne's room. Otto felt this was the best way.

On 17 November 1942, Fritz Pfeffer was the eighth person to go into hiding in the Secret Annex. Initially Anne liked her new room-mate, but soon found him to be increasingly irritating. He kept commenting on her behavior and also told on her to her mother. Anne found him to be a real pain.

Fortunately, there were also happy moments in the Secret Annex. For the first time in their lives, those in hiding celebrated

Victor Kugler giving the most recent news about what was happening outside of the hiding place.

Sinterklaas in early December. The helpers brought presents and wrote funny little poems. It was a fun evening of exchanging gifts.

Otto and Edith had planned in advance how they could spend the time. They had brought schoolbooks for Margot and Anne, and Otto gave lessons to the three youngsters. Every week the helpers brought new library books for everyone. Anne read book after book. Reading made her life less tedious.

Everyone in the group understood that they could only stay sane in the tiny space if they kept to a tight daily schedule. There were also strict rules for safety, because every sound could be dangerous. Below them in the company warehouse were people at work who knew nothing. They could not be allowed to find out that there were people hiding in the annex of the building.

The waste pipe from the toilet in the Secret Annex went straight down to the warehouse. Every morning there was a dangerous half-hour when the warehouse employees were already at work and the helpers had yet to arrive at the office.

Then those in hiding had to be extra quiet and not use the toilet. Once the helpers had arrived, the toilet could be used occasionally. The men working in the warehouse would assume that the sound came from the office waste pipe.

The people hiding in the annex would walk around in slippers all day and could only talk very softly during the day. They were happy when lunchtime came, as the warehouse workers would go home to eat. The helpers would often come to the hiding place for lunch and a chat. It was the nicest part of the day.

The helpers provided whatever was needed for those in hiding. For eight people, this meant a lot of groceries. Luckily they knew local shopkeepers they could trust, like the baker, the butcher and the vegetable grocer.

The dark winter passed slowly and spring came. Anne celebrated her fourteenth birthday on 12 June 1943. This was her first birthday in the Secret Annex and she had not been outside for almost a year. Anne was given lots of sweets and a big book about the mythology of Greece and Rome.

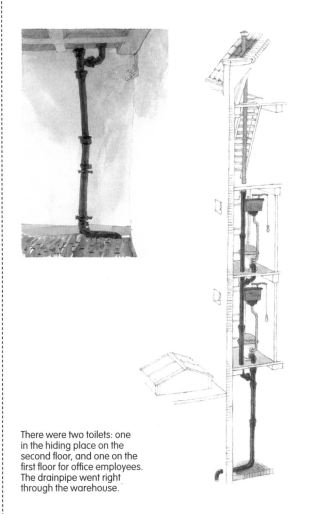

There were two toilets: one in the hiding place on the second floor, and one on the first floor for office employees. The drainpipe went right through the warehouse.

At night the people in hiding took turns using the washbasin and toilet. Anne was given from nine o'clock until half-past nine.

Was Anne Frank afraid in the Secret Annex?

In the Secret Annex, Anne was afraid of being discovered. She described this feeling in her diary: "One day we'd be laughing at the ridiculousness of the situation, but the next day and on many more days we would be frightened, and fear, tension and despair could be read on our faces." Anne also feared air raids, crashing airplanes and bombs. If a fire broke out, the people in hiding would have nowhere to go. Those bombs sometimes landed very close to them. In July 1943 a factory in Amsterdam Noord was targeted by Allied bombers. Trembling with fear, the group in the Secret Annex could do nothing but wait. The factory was not hit, but the bombs landed in a nearby residential suburb. More than 200 people were killed. In March 1944, Allied aircraft attacked the harbor of IJmuiden. The blasts could be heard in Amsterdam.

Bombardments of factories and the harbors of IJmuiden by Allied aircraft, 26 March 1944.

Some of the destroyed houses in Amsterdam-Nord after the bombardment of 15 July 1943.

Did the people in hiding get bored?

Anne wrote in her diary that she found Sundays particularly boring. That day there was no work going on in the building and so no helpers stopped by. The people in hiding tried to keep themselves as busy as they could. As well as all of the household jobs that needed to be done, like cooking food, washing up and cleaning, there was plenty of time to read and study. Anne's parents brought school books to the Secret Annex for Anne and Margot. The helpers provided books for reading, newspapers and magazines, and Bep Voskuijl applied for correspondence courses for Margot and Fritz Pfeffer using her own name. Margot and Anne also helped with the office work in the evenings and weekends.

Anne's favorite writer was Cissy van Marxveldt, author of the "Joop ter Heul" books. Anne read this series of books until they fell apart. It is to Kitty, one of the friends of the protagonist, to whom Anne ultimately addressed most of her diary letters.

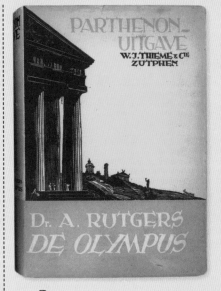

Anne celebrated her first birthday in hiding on 12 June 1943. She turned fourteen. Anne was given an interesting book about the mythology of Greece and Rome.

How did the people in hiding get new clothes and other things?

The helpers provided the group in the Annex with food, drinks, clothes, books and everything else they needed. Four of the five helpers worked in the office at the front of the building and kept Otto Frank's business going. Miep Gies and Bep Voskuijl did most of the daily grocery shopping. "Miep is just like a donkey, lugging stuff around," Anne wrote in her diary. Jo-hannes Kleiman and Victor Kugler were the managers of the company. They also helped out with any problems in the hiding place. For example, when there was an outbreak of fleas in the Secret Annex, Johannes Kleiman sprinkled powder to deal with them. Kleiman occasionally also brought along one of his daughter's books for Anne. Victor Kugler looked after the financial administration. He did not record some of the company income, so that this money could be used to buy what the people hiding in the Annex needed. Jan Gies, Miep's husband, did not work in the office, but also helped. He was involved in the resistance movement and looked after ration vouchers. These were necessary in order to be able to buy food and other scarce items.

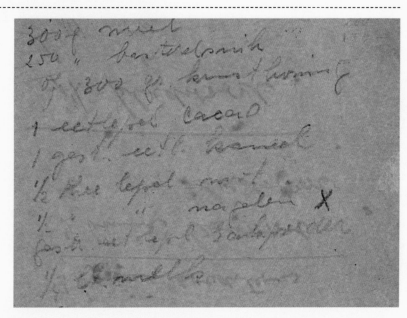

After the war, Miep found a shopping list for the butcher in her jacket pocket, written by Hermann van Pels. This is the back, on which Miep has written out a recipe for cake.

Anne's pictures

Initially Anne found her little room in the Secret Annex to be bare and cold. She made it nicer by sticking all kinds of pictures, postcards and advertising posters of Opekta, the product of her father's business, on the walls. Anne wanted to be a Hollywood film star, so she also covered an entire wall with pictures of film stars. However as she got older she became interested in other things and found some of the pictures on the wall a bit childish. Later, she wanted to study art history and become a journalist or writer. This is why Anne covered the older pictures with pictures of artworks from Leonardo da Vinci and Rembrandt.

One of the walls with Anne's pictures. An Opekta advertising poster still hung on the right.

It was discovered during restoration that there was another picture under this picture of a Michelangelo sculpture.

Anne glued Michelangelo's artwork on a picture of Rosemary and Priscilla Lane, famous Hollywood stars from that era.

Her father wrote a lovely birthday poem for her.

Anne actually liked writing best of all. Her diary was the most important, but she also wrote short stories and copied bits of text from books she found interesting. The short stories were about her time in school or things that happened in the Secret Annex, or were fairy tales she made up herself. She also began writing a novel called *Cady's Leven* (Cady's Life), and worked her father's life story into it. But Anne stopped with this after just a few chapters. She realized she did not yet have enough life experience.

Anne's passion for writing led to a major row with Fritz Pfeffer. Anne wanted to sit at the table in their room, but he did too. Fritz was learning Spanish because he wanted to emigrate to Chili after the war. Anne asked nicely if they could divide the time between them, but he did not want to do that. After asking a second time in vain, Anne asked her father to help. He talked with Fritz. Fritz finally relented: Anne could use the table two afternoons a week.

Anne found life difficult in the Secret Annex. She missed grandmother Holländer and wondered how things were for Hannah. She thought that Hannah and her other friends had been taken to a concentration camp ... Anne could not help them, she could only pray for them. Her belief in God was a comfort and a great source of strength.

Anne wrote her diary letters to Kitty, but she very much wanted to talk with a real person about what was on her mind. Maybe Peter? She would go to see him in his room in the evenings. Before long they were talking about everything, about their parents, their dreams and also about love. Anne had not expected that she would get on so well with this boring boy.

Peter and Anne fell in love. One evening when they were sitting close together in Peter's room, they kissed for the first time. Anne's first real kiss! Over the following weeks they would sit in the attic more often, because they felt more free up there. In Anne's opinion there was nothing nicer than lying in Peter's arms, but sometimes she had her doubts. Did it happen too quickly? And what would her parents think?

It was not easy for Anne and Fritz Pfeffer to share a small room.

Anne would occasionally peek through the curtains of the office at the front to see what was going on there.

She confided in her father, but did not tell him that they were in love. Otto Frank did not find this a problem at first, but later, he had his doubts. The situation in the Secret Annex was very different from how it would be in the normal world where Anne would be able to meet and go out with other boys and girls. This is why he felt that Anne should spend less time with Peter. What if they had a row? Life in the Secret Annex was already difficult enough.

Anne did not listen, she continued going to Peter. Otto told her off about this, and Anne was furious. She wrote her father a long letter. He could not treat her like she was a small child. She felt she had grown up more quickly than other girls and that this was due to her own merits. She wrote that her parents hadn't supported her in this. For Anne it was simple: her father should either trust her, or forbid her to go to Peter.

Otto was very hurt by this letter. He discussed it in depth with Anne. Why did she write such a letter? He and Edith had always supported her and always done their best for her. How did she get the idea that she had done everything alone? Anne realized she had gone too far and was deeply ashamed.

In spring 1944, the people in hiding heard on *Radio Oranje (Radio Orange)*, the Dutch radio broadcaster located in England, that diaries, letters and other documents would be gathered after the war. In this way, the hardships people suffered during the war would be recorded for posterity. The group immediately thought of Anne's diary and the news report gave Anne an idea. After considerable deliberation, in May she decided to write a real book about her time in the Secret Annex.

She used her diary entries as a source for this book, and made a new and more detailed version. She left out some parts because she found them too private, or not good enough. She also added new texts and had already thought of a title: *Het Achterhuis* (The Secret Annex). Her greatest dream was to be a journalist and a famous writer after the war.

In the meantime, her passion for Peter had cooled a bit and she distanced herself emotionally from him. He had not become the boyfriend she had longed for. She had

Anne would look out of the attic window to the large chestnut tree, the sky and the birds.

Peter's room had the stairs to the attic, which is why Anne called it the "walk-through room." She secretly envied Peter for his privacy.

The first floor

Just below the hiding place, on the first floor, is a kitchen and Otto Frank's office. During the weekend, some of the people in hiding would use the kitchen to wash themselves in a wash tub. It is the only place in the building with hot water.

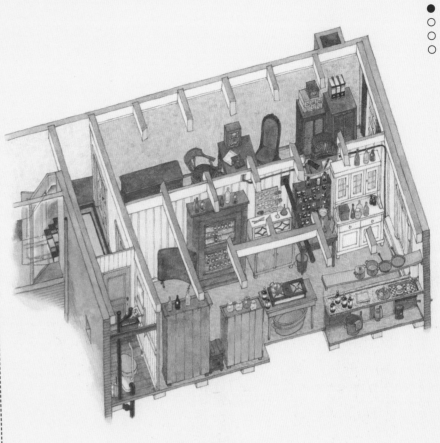

The office kitchen, 1954.

The second floor

On the second floor of the Secret Annex are two small rooms for the Frank family and Fritz Pfeffer. There is also a little room with a wash basin and toilet for the eight occupants.

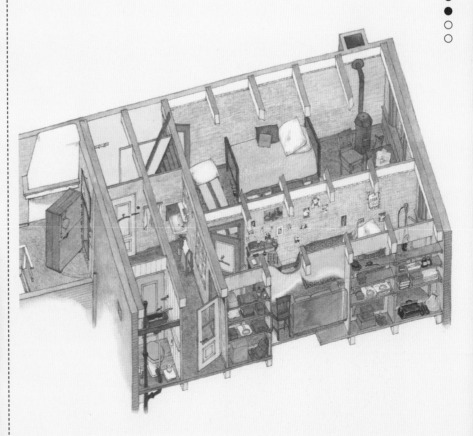

The room shared by Anne and Fritz Pfeffer, 1954.

The third floor

The Van Pels family lived on the third floor of the Secret Annex. Peter is the only one to have a room of his own. Auguste and Hermann van Pels' bedroom was also the communal living room and kitchen. A radio was brought here in the summer of 1943. In this way, they could follow the news in the evenings and weekends and listen to music.

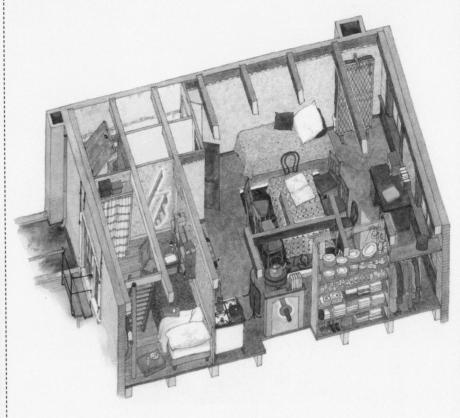

The communal living room and kitchen in the Secret Annex, 1954.

The attic

Anne would often go up to the attic alone, because the window there could be opened a little and she could get some fresh air. When Anne and Peter fell in love, the attic was the only place in the Secret Annex where they could be alone, away from the adults.

The attic of the Secret Annex, 1954.

hoped to be able to talk to him about her deepest thoughts and feelings, but this turned out not to be the case. Anne also thought it was a pity that her father did not tell her much about himself. It was because of this that she did not share her own thoughts with him.

On 6 June 1944 there was fantastic news. Thousands of Allied soldiers had crossed from Britain to France in ships and had landed on the French coast. They wanted to liberate all of the occupied countries and defeat Nazi Germany. Nazi Germany was caught in a vice: the Russians were attacking from the east, while the Americans, British and Canadians and other Allied forces were attacking from the west. Margot said that Anne might well be able to go back to school in October. Imagine!

In her diary, Anne paid less and less attention to the daily events in the Secret Annex and the news about the war. Instead, she thought more about herself. Why was she so different when other people were around? She appeared more superficial, but at the same time had a serious side that she herself found sweeter and more attractive. She

actually knew how she would have liked to be, but she couldn't manage to actually be this way.

Friday 4 August 1944 started out like every other day. The people in hiding got up, had breakfast and were quietly passing the time. Suddenly they heard the sound of tramping and clattering, and the bookcase that hid the entrance to the Secret Annex was pushed open.

Edith and Margot saw Victor Kugler appear. After him three men brandishing pistols entered the bedroom of Otto, Edith and Margot Frank. One of them wore a uniform of the German police (SD). Edith turned white, Margot started to cry quietly. Anne and Fritz Pfeffer came out of their room. They were discovered!

The two other men seemed to be Dutch plain-clothes policemen. They climbed the stairs and brought down the rest of the group. "*Wo sind Ihre Wertsachen?* (Where are your valuables?)" asked the German policeman. Otto Frank told him where the valuables were. The man grabbed Otto's briefcase and emptied it. This is where Anne

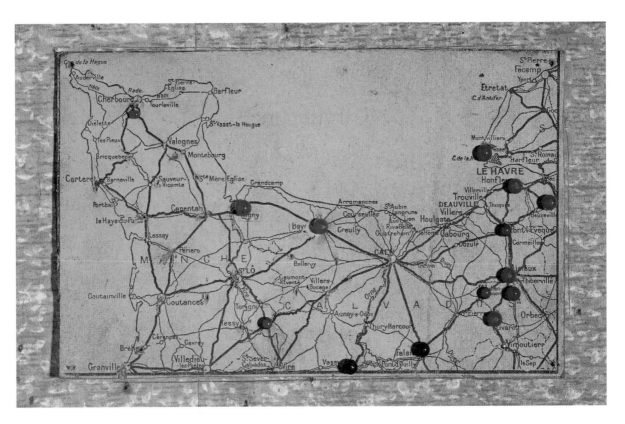

The people in hiding would keep track of the Allied advance with pins after the landing in France on 6 June 1944.

had kept her diary writings. She saw all her papers falling to the floor. Her diary! All her work! But the German police officer was not at all interested in Anne's diary and filled the empty briefcase with their jewellery and money.

"Get your things," he commanded, "everyone back here in five minutes." Defeated, the people in hiding began to pack their rucksacks. The German officer looked around and saw a gray trunk from the German army with Otto's name on it and his military rank: Reserve Lieutenant. "How did you get this?" he asked. Otto responded: "I was an officer in the German army ..." the policeman was surprised that Otto Frank, a Jew, fought with the German army in World War I. And as an officer too!

The two men started talking. Otto told the policeman, whose name was Karl Josef Silberbauer, that they had been hiding in the Secret Annex for over two years. Silberbauer wouldn't believe him at first. Otto asked Anne to stand at where he had marked her growth on the wallpaper so that Silberbauer could clearly see how much she had grown while in the Secret Annex.

One of the Dutch policemen organized a large vehicle to transport them. They had not counted on so many people, and the helpers Johannes Kleiman and Victor Kugler had to come along too. When the car arrived, they went down the stairs in a line. For Anne, this was the first time going outside after 761 days in hiding. It was a warm summer's day.

Neither Miep Gies nor Bep Voskuijl were arrested. When the agents entered the building, Kleiman sent Bep away immediately. She had to bring his wallet to an acquaintance. Bep could leave the building without any problem. To Miep, Kleiman said that she would have to keep pretending that she had known nothing about the people in hiding.

The people in hiding and two helpers had to get into a closed police vehicle. Otto Frank was horrified that Kleiman and Kugler were also arrested. Anyone who helped Jews was severely punished. Kleiman reassured him: "It was my choice and I don't regret it."

They were taken to the headquarters of the German police. There, everyone was interrogated: did they know any other addresses where people might be hiding?

After the arrest, Anne's diary papers lay strewn on the floor in the hiding place. They were found by Miep Gies and Bep Voskuijl.

"They were always together"

"I saw Anne Frank and Peter van Pels in Westerbork. They were always together. (...) Anne was beautiful in Westerbork, so radiant that it reflected on Peter. (...) Maybe I shouldn't say that her eyes glowed. But she had a warm glow about her, you understand? And she was so free in her movements and in her manner of looking that I wondered: 'Is she really happy, despite all that's happened?' She was happy in Westerbork, even though that's hard to understand, because it wasn't good in that camp."

Rosa de Winter
Source: Ernst Schnabel,
Footsteps of Anne Frank,
Southbank Publishing, 2015.

The card from the war with details about Anne Frank, from the Jewish Council of Amsterdam. On the upper right it says 8.8.44, Wbk (Westerbork camp), and B. 67 (Barrack 67). After the war, the Red Cross used cards like this to obtain information about what happened to deportees.

Marks showing growth

On the wallpaper in Otto and Edith's room there is a record of how much Margot and Anne grew while they were living in the Secret Annex. Margot did not grow very much, she was already sixteen when she went in hiding there. Her marks are on the right, she was measured twice. Anne was measured more often, she was still growing. The date was written down beside the marks, between 18 September 1942 and 29 July 1944 Anne grew 13 centimetres (5.12 inches).

What is the difference between a concentration camp and an extermination camp?

During the war the Nazis built a number of extermination camps in Poland, such as Belzec, Sobibor and Treblinka. Unlike the situation in the concentration camps, here the prisoners were killed soon after their arrival. In the Sobibor extermination camp, more than 30,000 Jewish men, women and children from the Netherlands died in the gas chambers. In the concentration camps most of the prisoners died because of hard labour, abuse, exhaustion and illness. There were also camps where both took place. Auschwitz is the most notorious example of a concentration and extermination camp.

Who betrayed Anne Frank?

The answer to this question is short: to this day, nobody knows. There were various investigations after the war, but nothing conclusive was ever discovered.

But that was not the case. The following day they were brought to the detention centre, where men and women were separated. The helpers were brought to a different jail. A few days later, in the early morning, the Frank family, the van Pels Family and Fritz Pfeffer were brought to Amsterdam Central Station. A train was waiting for them.

It was an ordinary train, but the door of every carriage was locked. Anne could not stay away from the window. For the first time in years, she was outside of Amsterdam. Mowed wheat fields, green woodlands and small villages flew past. After a couple of hours, the train arrived at Westerbork camp in Drenthe. Those who had been in hiding were categorised as "criminal cases."

Criminal cases were housed in a separate section of the camp. They had extra guards, were not allowed to have contact with other prisoners, were not allowed to send letters to family and friends and never received packages. Men and women were accommodated separately in the criminal barracks. They had to hand in their clothes and shoes and were given wooden shoes and blue overalls with red shoulder pieces to wear. A yellow star with the word *Jood* (Jew) was sewn onto the overalls. The men were given a cap.

There were more than 4,000 prisoners in Westerbork. All prisoners were required to work. They had to do things like sorting parts of aircraft wreckages that had been shot down. Edith, Margot and Anne were sent to work on the "batteries." They had to take old batteries apart, so that the parts could be reused, every day for ten hours. It was dirty work, because each battery contained a carbon rod and tar and dust. The prisoners became very dirty and the dust made them cough. However, they could talk among themselves while at work, which was some comfort.

In the evenings, the men and women were permitted to come together and Anne saw her father and Peter. After that long time hiding in the Secret Annex, everyone enjoyed talking to other people again. They heard the most recent news about the war: on 25 August the Allied forces had liberated Paris. When would the Netherlands be liberated? The prisoners were aware that

Jewish prisoners with their luggage at the train in Westerbork transit camp, 1943.

A photograph of Westerbork. 107,000 Jewish prisoners were transported by train to concentration and extermination camps in the east. Only 5,000 of them returned after the war.

Westerbork was a "transit" camp: trains full of prisoners often departed from Westerbork to Eastern Europe. Prisoners considered to be criminals usually had to leave with the next transport.

On 2 September 1944, a list of names of those prisoners who would be put on the train to the east the following day was read out in the criminal barracks. Most of the prisoners in the criminal barracks would have to go, including the eight who had hidden in the Secret Annex. More than a thousand men, women and children had to prepare to leave. Young, old, sick, healthy …. None of that mattered: whoever was on the list had to go.

The following morning the prisoners had to hand in their caps, overalls and wooden shoes and their own clothes were returned to them. They walked to the train that was waiting for them. It was not a passenger train, but a train for transporting cattle. Each carriage held about seventy prisoners and there were two barrels: one with drinking water and an empty barrel which would have to serve as a toilet. Otto, Edith, Margot and Anne were together in the same carriage. The door was pushed closed and bolted from the outside. The guards traveled with them in separate passenger carriages.

The prisoners had no idea where they were going and how long the journey would take. The drinking water was gone very quickly and the stink of the toilet barrel was almost unbearable. Everyone clung to each other in exhaustion, as the carriage was too tightly packed to lie down. Along the way, the train was stopped and the guards robbed the prisoners, taking all of their money and jewelry.

While traveling through the Netherlands, a group of eight prisoners in another carriage made a desperate attempt to escape. They had smuggled a drill and a saw from the camp workshop, and used these to saw a hole in the back wall of their carriage, close to the floor. One by one, they dropped from the moving train onto the rails. As a result, three of them were seriously injured and ended up in hospital. Ultimately seven of them would survive the war, through the help of the Resistance. The train kept moving.

Part of the list of names of the transport of 3 September 1944, including Otto, Edith, Margot and Anne Frank. All eight people who had hidden in the Secret Annex were on the same transport to Auschwitz in occupied Poland.

The sign for the train that went between Westerbork and Auschwitz. It also says: "No carriage is to be uncoupled: train must return to Westerbork intact."

The selection in Auschwitz

Jewish men and women standing separately from each other on the platform of Auschwitz-Birkenau. Women with children stood on the right, the men on the left. Nazi doctors stood ready to select the prisoners: those who would have to work and those who would be exterminated immediately. Thirteen-year-old Irene Fogel is second from the left. She was selected to work. Along with her oldest sister Serena, she is the only one from a Jewish family of eight to survive Auschwitz.

This photograph was taken by the Nazi photographer who took identity photos of prisoners in Auschwitz who would be put to work. In almost 200 photographs, he recorded the arrival of a group of Jews from Hungary during May or June, 1944.

What happened after Johannes Kleiman and Victor Kugler were arrested?

Helpers Johannes Kleiman and Victor Kugler were arrested on 4 August 1944 along with those who had been hiding in the Secret Annex. After being interrogated by the police, they were brought to prison. They were sent to camp Amersfoort a few weeks later. This was where mainly political opponents and members of the Resistance movement were held. Johannes Kleiman was sick, he had stomach problems. He was released through pressure from the Red Cross. In March 1945 Victor Kugler was selected for a group of 600 Dutch men who would have to walk to Germany to work there. The column was shot at by Allied aircraft close to the German border and Kugler managed to escape. He was able to go into hiding until the Netherlands was liberated in May 1945. All of the helpers survived the war.

A large group of prisoners from the Amersfoort camp being transported to the Neuengamme concentration camp in northern Germany, 11 October 1944.

Russian soldiers approaching

German soldiers in their positions on a hill at the eastern front where they fought against the Soviet army in September 1944. On the horizon, the results of grenade attacks are visible. The German army lost the Battle of Stalingrad in early 1943. In this battle for the city, which lasted several months, 470,000 soldiers died, all of them German. 100,000 German soldiers became prisoners of war, and only 5,000 of these survived the war. The Battle of Stalingrad was a turning point in World War II. The German army could not withstand the Russians, who kept sending new troops and weapons to the front. At the end of 1944, parts of eastern Poland were once again in the hands of the Soviet forces.

What is the Holocaust?

The Holocaust is another word for the persecution of Jews by Nazi Germany in the period 1933-1945. The Nazis and their collaborators murdered six million Jews during World War II. They were killed in gas chambers, shot dead behind the front line, or died of exhaustion from the hard forced labor and the poor hygiene prevalent in the camps. Most of the victims were from Eastern Europe: three million Jews were from Poland and one million from Russia. This genocide of the European Jews was called the Holocaust. Because the word *Holocaust* actually means "burnt sacrifice," some people prefer to use the word Shoah. Shoah is the Hebrew word for "destruction" or "destructive whirlwind."

After the liberation, Russian soldiers found a large mountain of spectacles that had belonged to prisoners murdered in Auschwitz

After three days, the train suddenly stopped. It was the middle of the night. The doors were pushed open. *"Aussteigen, schnell, schneller"* (Get out, quickly, faster), screamed men in blue-gray striped prison clothes waving clubs. These were *"Kapos,"* prisoners who were forced to work as guards. "Leave your luggage on the train." On the platform were German soldiers with whips and large dogs. The group had arrived at Auschwitz-Birkenau concentration camp. What would happen to them now?

In spring 1944, the Nazis made a propaganda film about a train that departed from Westerbork. This is an image from that film. The girl's name is Settela Steinbach. She came from a Sinti family. 250 Sinti and Roma gypsies were deported from Westerbork to Auschwitz. Settela's father was the only member of the family to survive.

A train with prisoners is ready to depart Westerbork transition camp.

Chapter 5

Anne's death

Men and women prisoners were separated on the Auschwitz-Birkenau platform. They had to line up in rows of five. Girls and boys younger than fifteen had to stand with their mothers. A Nazi doctor checked all the prisoners and sent them either left or right.

Edith, Margot, Anne and Auguste van Pels were sent to the same side. They walked with other female prisoners to another building, where they had to wait for hours. There, they had to hand in everything they had brought with them, and take off their clothes. They were also registered and an identification number was tattooed on their arms.

The women were shaved bald and then put under a shower. Finally, they could drink some water. After the shower they were given random clothes and shoes, because there were no more striped prison clothes available. One would get a summer's dress, the other a thick woollen dress, two left shoes, worn shoes, the guards did not care. Then they were sent to another barrack, a large shed with wooden bunkbeds.

There the women finally learned the awful truth. All Jewish men, women and children from their train that had been sent to the other side, had died in the camp gas chambers. The gas chambers were large rooms with closable openings in the ceiling. The Nazis had set these up to look like bathrooms. The guards would throw down pellets of poisonous gas (Zyklon B) among the prisoners through the openings in the ceiling. As soon as these pellets came into contact with air, they would change into lethal gas. Very quickly everyone in that room would be dead. The bodies were then incinerated in large ovens, the crematoria.

Prisoners searching through the luggage of Hungarian Jews for valuable items. A German soldier is supervising, Auschwitz, May or June 1944.

Jewish mothers and children going to the gas chamber, Auschwitz, May or June 1944.

Victims of the Nazi terror

According to the Nazis, in addition to the Jews, there were some other groups of people who also needed to be removed or even exterminated. And that did happen. In Europe, millions of people were killed by the Nazis and their collaborators because of their origin, religion, handicap, sexual orientation and/or political preferences. We will never know the exact numbers. This is an estimate of the number of deaths caused by the Nazi terror:

- Jews: 6,000,000
- Russians: 9,000,000 (not including Jews)
- Poles: 1,800,000 (not including Jews)
- Roma and Sinti (gypsies): 200,000
- Serbians: 312,000
- Handicapped people: 250,000
- Homosexuals: hundreds, possibly thousands of victims.
- Jehovah's Witnesses: 1,900
- Criminals and "asocial individuals": 70,000
- Political opponents of the Nazis: number of victims unknown

Source: www.ushmm.org

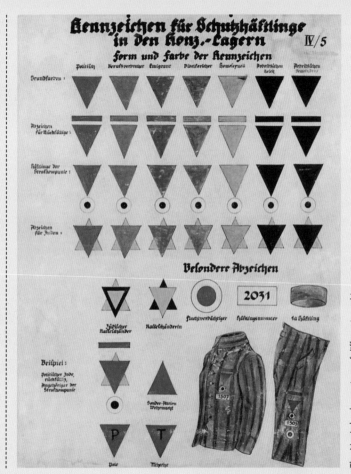

The Nazis had a system of different markings for each group of prisoners in a concentration camp. For example, homosexuals had a pink triangle on their uniform, while Jehovah's Witnesses had a purple one.

"Totally exhausted"

"Edith became sick, she had a high fever. I wanted her to go to the infirmary barracks. But the fear of being gassed was too great, as every week Dr. Mengele visited the infirmary barracks to look for women who he thought were too thin to continue living. Despite everything, I brought Edith there. She had a fever of 41 degrees and was immediately admitted to the infirmary." Rosa de Winter also became sick and was admitted to a different barrack for sick prisoners, where, after a while, she saw Edith again. "Some new patients came in one morning. I suddenly recognized Edith, she came from a different department. She was only a shadow of her former self. She died a few days later, totally exhausted."

Rosa de Winter
Source: Rosa de Winter-Levy, *Aan de gaskamer ontsnapt!*, Misset, 1945.

Shortly after the end of the war in 1945, the booklet *Aan de gaskamer ontsnapt!* by Rosa de Winter-Levy was published. In it she tells of the death of Edith Frank in Auschwitz.

"I survived because of that."

"I was in Auschwitz and feeling very despondent and unable to do anything anymore. They had beaten me and because of this I was very (...) down and intimidated. It was a Sunday and I said 'I can't get up.' Then my comrades (....) said: 'No, you can't, you must get up, otherwise you are lost.' They went to a Dutch doctor who was working with the German doctor. He came to me in the barracks and said: 'Get up and come to the infirmary early tomorrow. I'll talk to the German doctor and make sure you are admitted.' And that's what happened. I survived because of that."

Otto Frank
Source: Otto Frank in the German documentary *Laßt mich so sein, wie ich will*, Südwestfunk, 1979.

Otto Frank in the manager's office of his company, 1954. He is showing his camp number from Auschwitz: B-9174.

A journal from Bergen-Belsen

Just like Anne's friend Hannah Goslar, Ruth Wiener was also a prisoner in the *Sternlager* of Bergen-Belsen. This was a section of the concentration camp where Jews were held who the Nazis wanted to exchange for German soldiers who were prisoners of war. Ruth knew Margot and Anne from the Jewish Lyceum. She wrote down all kinds of things in her own journal between 1943 and 1945. On 20 December 1944 she noted down: "Margot and Anne Frank are in another part of the camp."

The new prisoners were kept in a separate part of Auschwitz-Birkenau in order to learn the rules of the camp. The camp managers used other prisoners to supervise them. These "*Kapos*" were strict and would beat their fellow prisoners with clubs. Every day the new prisoners had to cut sods of turf and carry heavy rocks. They also had to stand to attention for hours: everyone had to stand in line to be counted. The food in the camp was bad: watery soup, a small piece of bread, sometimes with a little margarine or sausage, and weak coffee.

Because of these awful conditions, Anne and Margot contracted scabies, an illness brought about by mites, little creatures that cause itchy bumps. There was a special "scabies barracks" and Margot and Anne had to go there. Edith helped them as much as she could. However, because of the risk of contagion, she was not allowed inside, so she dug a hole under the barracks wall. In this way she managed to slip her daughters the occasional piece of bread.

There were regular "selections." In one selection, the Nazi doctors would send the women who were sick to the gas chamber; in another they would look to see which women were still suitable to work in Nazi Germany. These prisoners were sent to another camp. There was one such selection at the end of October 1944. Edith Frank was designated to join the group that would stay in Auschwitz-Birkenau. Anne, Margot and Auguste van Pels were to go away with the transport.

After a gruelling journey of a few days they arrived at Bergen-Belsen, a concentration camp in the north of Nazi Germany. There was not enough room here for so many extra prisoners, so they were initially housed in large tents. But a few days later there was a heavy storm and the tents were blown down. Now they were forced to move into the barracks, which were already overcrowded. Each barrack had hundreds of women propped up against each other.

Bergen-Belsen consisted of different sections which were separated by barbwire fences. Armed soldiers in watchtowers kept an eye on everyone. The prisoners were not allowed go near the barbwire fences, but they did in secret anyway when it was dark. They hoped to find out if any friends or family members had arrived at the camp.

A section of the Bergen-Belsen concentration camp after liberation. The wooden buildings are the barracks.

Jewish prisoners after their registration, Auschwitz, May or June 1944.

A barracks at Bergen-Belsen.

In the section known as the "Sternlager" there were Jews who the Nazis wanted to exchange with the Allied forces for German prisoners of war. One of these prisoners was Anne's friend Hannah Goslar. Hannah heard that Anne was also in Bergen-Belsen. She didn't understand. Hadn't Anne fled to Switzerland?

One evening Hannah managed to speak to Anne. Crying, they stood on either side of the barbwire fence, unable to see each other. Anne said that her parents were dead and that she had almost nothing to eat. Hannah found some food and clothes for her, which she brought the next time. She threw the package over the barbwire fence, and then heard Anne screaming. Someone else had caught the package and had run away with it. A few days later she threw another package over the fence. Luckily Anne got that one. They were able to talk a few times, until Anne and Margot had to move to another place within the camp.

Nannie Blitz, a classmate from the Jewish Lyceum, also saw Anne in Bergen-Belsen. Anne was very thin, was covered in lice and had wrapped a blanket around herself.

Anne told her about their time hiding in the Secret Annex, the betrayal and that she had come to Bergen-Belsen via Auschwitz.

Anne and Nannie talked regularly until Anne came down with typhus, as did Margot. This is an extremely contagious disease that is spread by lice. Thousands of prisoners in the camp suffered from it. They had high fever, skin rashes, headaches and needed to vomit.

Rachel van Amerongen was another prisoner in Bergen-Belsen who could remember Margot and Anne. After the war, she said that Anne and Margot looked absolutely ravaged by typhus. They were constantly cold, because they lay in their barrack beside the door that never stopped opening and closing. Margot was the first to succumb, and Anne died a few days later. It was February 1945.

In February Auguste van Pels was transported from Bergen-Belsen to Raguhn. She was one of around 500 prisoners who were selected to work in a factory for aircraft parts. In April 1945, the American troops came so close to the camp that the

Two Jewish children after they had been liberated in Bergen-Belsen camp. They suffered from typhus but had been bathed and given clean clothes.

Liberated prisoners in Bergen-Belsen, April 1945.

A stone memorial

Margot and Anne Frank died of typhus in February 1945 in the Bergen-Belsen concentration camp, just like thousands of other prisoners. After the camp was liberated in April 1945, all of the dead were buried in mass graves. It is not known where exactly Margot and Anne lie buried. In 1999 – Anne would have been seventy years old that year – a stone memorial was erected on the grounds of the former concentration camp.

The fate of the people in hiding

This map shows where the seven fugitives from the Secret Annex who perished met their ends.

Auschwitz: Hermann van Pels and Edith Frank
Neuengamme: Fritz Pfeffer
Bergen-Belsen: Margot and Anne Frank
Mauthausen: Peter van Pels
During a transport between Raguhn and

Theresienstadt: Auguste van Pels
Otto Frank was the only one to return from the concentration and extermination camps.

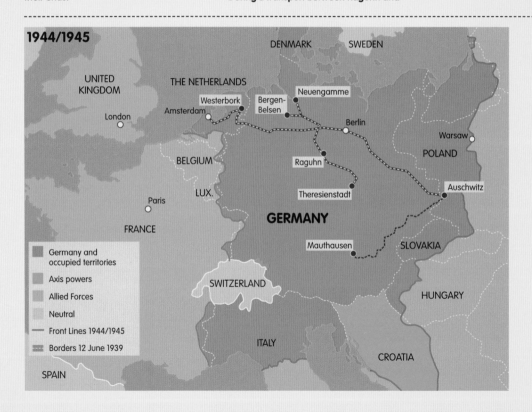

1944/1945

SWEDEN
DENMARK
UNITED KINGDOM
THE NETHERLANDS
Neuengamme
Westerbork
Bergen-Belsen
London
Amsterdam
Berlin
Warsaw
POLAND
BELGIUM
Raguhn
LUX.
Theresienstadt
Auschwitz
Paris
GERMANY
FRANCE
Mauthausen
SLOVAKIA
SWITZERLAND
HUNGARY
ITALY
CROATIA
SPAIN

Germany and occupied territories
Axis powers
Allied Forces
Neutral
Front Lines 1944/1945
Borders 12 June 1939

camp leaders decided to evacuate. All prisoners were put on the train to Theresienstadt concentration camp, without food or water. Many of them died during this journey, including Auguste van Pels.

What was the fate of the men from the Secret Annex? After arriving at Auschwitz, Otto Frank, Herman and Peter van Pels and Fritz Pfeffer were put to work in a gravel quarry outside of the camp. They had to fill carts with shingle. Hermann van Pels hurt his hand doing this heavy work. The next day he remained behind in the barracks. When the Nazi doctor came by to check on him, he was taken away. Otto and Peter van Pels saw him being marched away in a group of selected men. Hermann van Pels was killed in one of the gas chambers in early October 1944.

Fritz Pfeffer was sent off on a transport in another selection, and ended up in the Neuengamme concentration camp near Hamburg in November. The work was back-breaking and prisoners were given very little to eat. Fritz Pfeffer died of exhaustion and sickness on 20 December 1944.

Peter van Pels ended up working in the post-collection point in Auschwitz. Some prisoners were allowed to receive post and packages. Some packages contained food and Peter was sometimes able to steal some of these. He shared the extra food with Otto Frank.

When the Russian army was approaching Auschwitz-Birkenau in January 1945, the guards cleared the camp. They destroyed as many documents as they could and blew up the gas chambers and crematoria. Prisoners who could still walk were made to leave with the guards. Peter van Pels was one of them. Otto Frank was weak, he had been sick in the infirmary for weeks. He tried to persuade Peter to hide somewhere, but Peter decided he would go. He was convinced he would survive. Otto was afraid that the sick who remained behind would be shot, but the rapid advance of the Russian troops put the Nazis on the run.

After a long and difficult journey, Peter van Pels arrived at Mauthausen concentration camp. He was sent on to another camp in the area: Melk. There, the prisoners worked on the construction of an underground

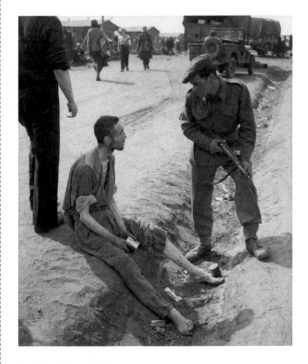

English soldier and prisoner of war Louis Bonerguer in conversation with an English soldier who liberated Bergen-Belsen camp in April 1945. Parachutist Bonerguer was captured by German soldiers in the occupied territory in 1941 and was imprisoned in Bergen-Belsen.

Survivors of Bergen-Belsen by a mountain of shoes, April 1945. When Bergen-Belsen was still a concentration camp, the prisoners had to take apart old shoes for reuse.

factory for tank and aircraft parts. They had to drill out hallways, remove soil, make beams to support tunnels and load and unload building materials.

It was dangerous work and there were frequent accidents. The prisoners were in rags and sometimes no longer had shoes. They were given hardly any food, in the end there wasn't even bread. In early April, the Russian army advanced so close that the guards evacuated Melk camp. Peter returned, sick, to Mauthausen, were he ended up in the infirmary. It was full beyond capacity and there were no medicines. Prisoners sometimes had to lie four to a bed. Mauthausen camp was liberated on 5 May, but for Peter this liberation came too late. He was so sick and weak that he died a few days later on 10 May 1945.

For Otto Frank, the liberation came just in time. Russian soldiers entered Auschwitz concentration camp on 27 January 1945, where they encountered as many as 7,000 prisoners still alive, including Otto Frank. After he was liberated, he wrote that it was truly a miracle that he was still alive.

Peter van Pels' card from the administration of Mauthausen concentration camp. On the front are his personal details, on the back is his profession *Tischler* (furniture maker) and where he was imprisoned.

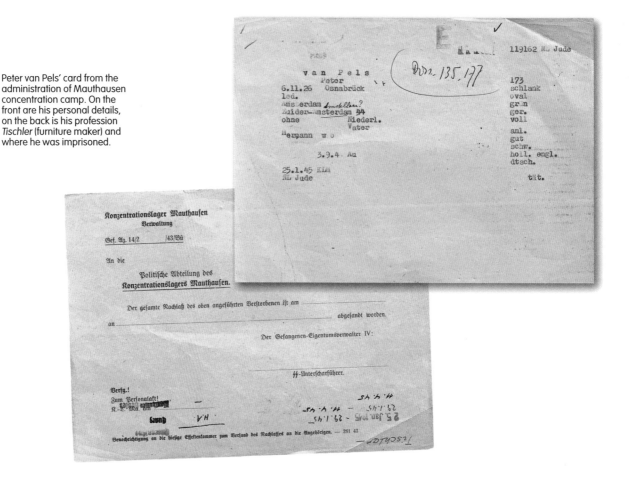

After the liberation of Bergen-Belsen

A little boy walks through the liberated Bergen-Belsen concentration camp in May 1945. The sides of the road were littered with the corpses of dead prisoners. The photograph was taken by the British war photographer George Rodger and published in the famous American *Life* magazine in 1945. An uncle of the little boy who was living in the United States recognized him. He was Simon (Sieg) Maandag, a Jewish child from Amsterdam. The uncle ensured that Simon was reunited with his mother and sister in the Netherlands. George Rodger was the first to take photographs of the liberated Bergen-Belsen concentration camp. After all that he saw, Rodger decided to stop working as a war photographer.

Otto's return journey

Otto Frank kept his possessions in this little bag. He kept a precise record of the return journey to the Netherlands in a notebook, and also noted down important events, such as Hitler's death, the liberation of the Netherlands and the capitulation of Nazi Germany. Otto Frank no longer had any personal identity documents. After arriving in Marseilles, France, he had to complete a *Carte de Rapatrié* (repatriation card) with his personal details. He provided the address of Jan and Miep Gies in Amsterdam, because that was where he wanted to go.

Chapter 6

Otto's return and Anne's diary

Now that he was free, Otto Frank only wanted to know two things: were Edith, Margot and Anne still alive, and where were they? He had not seen them since they had arrived on the platform at Auschwitz-Birkenau. Otto slowly regained his strength. As soon as he was sufficiently recovered, there was nothing he wanted more than to return to the Netherlands. But that was not possible, because there was still a lot of fighting going on in many countries.

In March 1945 Otto Frank traveled with a group of around 800 survivors to Odessa (Soviet Union). Along the way he met Rose de Winter, who had also been in Auschwitz. She told him that Edith had died in the camp and that Margot and Anne were taken away. She did not know where they went.

In Odessa, on the Black Sea, the group had to wait a month for a ship that would be sailing in the direction of the Netherlands. There, they learned that Nazi Germany had capitulated. The Netherlands was a free country again! On 21 May, they traveled by the ship the *Monowai*, to Marseilles in France. From there, Otto continued on to Amsterdam over land. The journey took a long time, as there wasn't much transport available and in the Netherlands itself the bridges were destroyed. He finally returned to Amsterdam on 3 June.

Otto immediately went to Jan and Miep Gies. They were so happy to see him and mourned Edith's death with him. They told him that Johannes Kleiman and Victor Kugler had survived the war. They all hoped that

"Hitler dead" is on the front of the American publication *The Stars and Stripes*, a newspaper for American military, 2 May 1945.

Russian soldiers liberated the Auschwitz concentration and extermination camp on 27 January 1945. Otto was in the infirmary. He weighed just 50 kilos, about 110 pounds.

Margot and Anne would return. On 12 June, Otto could not help thinking about Anne all day, as that would have been her 16th birthday. Was she still alive? And Margot?

Otto would regularly go to Amsterdam Central Station to ask people returning from the camps if they had seen Anne and Margot. He also checked the Red Cross lists. The survivors would mark the names of those who had died with little crosses. One day he saw crosses behind Anne and Margot's names. Otto went looking for the people who had made those crosses. They were Janny and Lientje Brilleslijper. They had been imprisoned in Bergen-Belsen and told him that Margot and Anne had died of typhus.

Otto Frank was devastated. Not only his wife, but his children were dead. When Miep heard that Margot and Anne were not coming back, she went to her desk: in a drawer she had kept the papers from Anne's diary for all that time. Miep and Bep had found them on the floor of the Secret Annex after everyone had been arrested.
Miep had hoped to be able to return them to Anne after the war. Now she gave the entire package to Anne's father.

Otto could not read the diaries right away, his grief was too much. But when he did start reading them a month later, he found it very difficult to stop. He discovered a completely different side to his daughter Anne: her serious side. She had described their time in the Secret Annex so precisely, so well, and with great humor. He had forgotten so much of that.

He typed out some of the texts for family and friends. What should he do with these? Anne herself had thought she would like to publish a book with the title *Het Achterhuis* (The (Secret) Annex). Otto decided to make this wish come true and he compiled a book from Anne's texts. But it was difficult to find a publisher. Many people in the Netherlands did not want to be reminded of the war. They wanted to look to the future and forget the horrors of war as quickly as possible.

Through a friend of Otto's, the manuscript ended up in the hands of Jan and Annie Romein, two well-known historians. Jan Romein read it in one sitting and was very impressed. He wrote an article praising it that was printed on the front page of the

Otto and Fritzi Frank on their wedding day, 10 November 1953. From left to right: Jan Gies, Johannes Kleiman, Fritzi Frank, Otto Frank, Johanna Kleiman and Miep Gies.

Otto (center) a few months after his return from Auschwitz, with the helpers who worked at the office. Left to right: Miep Gies, Johannes Kleiman, Victor Kugler and Bep Voskuijl, 1945.

How did Anne Frank become so famous?

There are a few possible reasons for this:
- Anne had a great talent for writing.
- Anne was an innocent young girl who was murdered merely for being Jewish.
- Otto Frank survived the camps and dedicated himself to publishing and distributing Anne's diary.
- You can actually visit the Secret Annex, the place where the diary was written.
- There are many photos of Anne Frank and her family.
- Anne's story has become famous all over the world through plays, films and documentaries.
- The diary is about a young girl growing up, who, when in hiding was thinking about herself and the world around her.

A year before he died, Otto Frank talked about this in an interview: "Every day I still get post from readers all over the world (...), places like Australia, South Africa, Japan or America, and that is the special thing about Anne's diary. Because of this, I can truly say that it is a 'document humain' (document of humanity). It is human and touches people, no matter where they live."

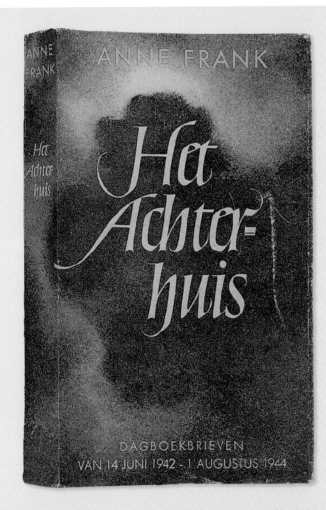

Het Achterhuis (The Secret Annex) was published on 25 June1947. Designer Helmut Salden created the cover: a sun disappearing behind dark clouds.

Statement

In the summer of 1945, Otto Frank met sisters Janny and Lientje Brilleslijper in Amsterdam. They had been imprisoned in Bergen-Belsen concentration camp. Janny and Lientje told Otto that Margot and Anne had died there. At Otto Frank's request, Lientje (Rebekka) Brilleslijper, in November 1945 made an official statement that Margot and Anne Frank had died in the Bergen-Belsen concentration camp at the "end of February or beginning of March 1945." The exact date of their deaths is not known.

In August 1945 Otto Frank placed an appeal in the newspaper Het Vrije Volk. Otto was searching for people who could tell him anything about Anne and Margot.

Why is there no furniture in the Secret Annex?

Shortly after the people in hiding were arrested on 4 August 1944, the Secret Annex was emptied. This had been ordered by the occupying forces. The furniture and other items were probably sent to Nazi Germany. After the arrest, helpers Miep Gies and Bep Voskuijl could only save a few personal belongings of those who had been in hiding, such as Anne's diary. The Secret Annex became a museum in 1960. Otto Frank was asked if the Secret Annex should be re-furnished, but he didn't want that. In a speech he said: "Everything was taken away during the war, I want to keep it this way."

Otto Frank and Johannes Weiss (right) beside two models of the hiding place, 1961. In order to give visitors to the Anne Frank House a better impression of the living conditions for the people in hiding, Otto had Johannes Weiss design these two models.

What punishment was given to the Nazis who worked in the camps?

After World War II there were several trials for Nazi war crimes. The first trial began in September 1945 against the Commander and guards of the Bergen-Belsen concentration camp. 45 suspects appeared before the Judge:

- Eleven of them received the death penalty.
- One was given a life sentence.
- Eighteen received prison sentences of between one and fifteen years.
- Fifteen were acquitted.

Many other Nazis have never been punished.

The arrest of Josef Kramer, commander of the Bergen-Belsen camp, by British Allied troops, 15 April 1945. Josef Kramer was given the death penalty in November and executed on 13 December 1945.

newspaper *Het Parool*. "When I had finished reading it, it was night and I was amazed that the light was still burning, that bread and tea were still available, that I did not hear the roar of aircraft overhead or the marching of soldiers' boots on the street, I was so caught up and brought back to that unreal world that is now almost a year behind us."

Shortly after this, the Contact Publishing Company got in touch with Otto Frank. They wanted to publish Anne's diary. In 1947, two years after the war, *Het Achterhuis* was published with a foreword by Annie Romein. The first issue was around 3,000 copies. After a few years, there were translations into German, French and English.

The foreword of the American publication was written by Eleanor Roosevelt, wife of the American President. She wrote: "This is an astonishing book. Written by a young girl—and young people are not afraid to tell the truth—it is one of the wisest and most moving commentaries of war and the effect of war on humans that I have ever read." When there was a play in the United States, and later on a film made about *The Secret*

Annex, the diary became famous all over the world.

Ultimately Otto Frank did not want to live in Amsterdam any longer, because for him there were so many memories attached to the Secret Annex. "I can't bear to see it any more," he said in an interview. In 1952 he moved to Basel (Switzerland), where his mother and sister Leni and Leni's family still lived. A year later he married Fritzi Geiringer, who along with her daughter Eva had also survived Auschwitz.

Otto Frank spent the rest of his life promoting Anne's diary. More and more people wanted to see the place where Anne wrote her diary for themselves. Funds were collected to conserve the hiding place and open it to the public. The Anne Frank House opened its doors on 3 May 1960. The hiding place became a museum. Naturally Otto Frank was present at the opening. Moved to tears, he said: "I beg your forgiveness, I cannot speak any longer, but the thought of what happened here is too much for me." He then thanked everyone briefly but very sincerely for their support.

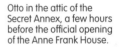

Otto in the attic of the Secret Annex, a few hours before the official opening of the Anne Frank House.

In 1954 there was a plan to demolish Prinsengracht 263. Thanks to a special fund-raising drive, the front house and the Annex were saved. Rob Witsel and Hans Meenke (right) stayed in the Secret Annex for one night to prevent people from damaging it or taking anything away. Eventually both the front of the building and the Annex were restored. The Anne Frank House opened to visitors on 3 May 1960.

Otto and Fritzi received thousands of letters from all over the world from readers who were very moved by Anne's diary. They corresponded with some of these for many years, and became friends. Otto felt that Anne had given him the task of devoting himself to reconciliation and human rights. He was to fight discrimination and prejudice. Otto's belief was that everyone should do this. Shortly before he died in 1980, he wrote: "Young people in particular want to know how these terrible events could ever have come about. I will answer them as best I can. At the end I often write: 'I hope that Anne's book will stay with you in your later life, so that you will work for cooperation and peace, as far as this is possible in your immediate environment.'"

Otto and Fritzi Frank with Eva and her children in Basel, 1967.

Youth conference at the Anne Frank House, 1968. Otto wanted to bring young people from all over the world together in Amsterdam for lectures and courses about current affairs such as conflicts, racism and discrimination. He hoped to promote freedom, democracy and equal rights through these discussions among young people.

Human rights

This is Eleanor Roosevelt, wife of American President Franklin Roosevelt. She is holding the Universal Declaration of Human Rights, which she and people from various other countries set out for the United Nations. The United Nations is the organization that was set up in 1945 to prevent war and improve cooperation among countries. Human rights must ensure that everyone everywhere can always live without fear and in freedom. Examples of human rights are: protection against discrimination, the right to a fair trial and freedom to express an opinion. On 10 December 1948, during a general meeting of the United Nations, this list of thirty human rights was adopted.

Anne's friends

Kitty Egyedi, Hannah Goslar and Jaqueline van Maarsen at the opening of the exhibition *Nu ben ik dus vijftien* (Now I am fifteen), about the life of Anne Frank in the Anne Frank House, October 2012. Anne's friend Jacqueline is not in the birthday photo from 1939 because they did not meet each other until later. Jacqueline survived the war because her mother managed to arrange official papers on which it stated that she was "non-Jewish." This meant that the Nazis considered Jacqueline not Jewish and she did not have to go into hiding.

Anne's friends

At the start of this book you see a photo of Anne Frank's tenth birthday: nine little girls in a row in Amsterdam, 1939. How did life turn out for Anne's friends?

Juultje Ketellapper was Jewish. She was arrested with her parents and sister on 20 June 1943 and brought to Westerbork transit camp. On 6 July the Ketellapper family was put on a transport to Sobibor. In this extermination camp, all prisoners were killed in the gas chambers immediately after arrival. More than 34,000 Jewish men, women and children from the Netherlands were murdered there. Juultje, along with her parents and sisters, died there on 9 July 1943. She had just turned fifteen.

Sanne Ledermann was also Jewish, and like Juultje, arrested with her parents in Amsterdam on 20 June 1943. They were also taken to Westerbork transit camp. Sanne turned fifteen there. On 16 November 1943, they were taken to Auschwitz-Birkenau. Sanne and her parents died in the gas chambers immediately after arriving there on 19 November 1943.

Kitty Egyedi's parents were also Jewish, they were originally from Hungary. Kitty also ended up in Westerbork with her parents. She was there at the same time as Anne, but they did not see each other. On 4 September 1944 Kitty and her parents were put on a train to Theresienstadt concentration camp. The Egyedi family survived that camp. After the war Kitty became a dentist, just like her father.

Mary Bos did not experience the war in the Netherlands. She and her parents and brothers emigrated to New York shortly before the war broke out. Her father Arie was a Dutch billiards champion and her American mother Catherine was a billiards champion too in the United States. Mary's father was Jewish, her mother was not. Mary remained living in the United States.

Martha van den Berg, Iet Swillens and Lucie van Dijk remained in Amsterdam throughout the war. Martha was an eye-witness to the razzias on Jewish residents. Lucie's parents were members of the NSB and Lucie herself joined the *Jeugdstorm*, the NSB youth organisation. In 1942 Lucie and her father cancelled their respective memberships. All three girls survived the *Hongerwinter* (the winter of starvation), as the winter of 1944/1945 is known, when more than 20,000 people in the occupied Netherlands died through lack of food. After the war, Lucie worked at a printer's. Martha studied physics and became a teacher, and Iet Swillens taught in vocational education.

Hannah Goslar survived the Bergen-Belsen concentration camp. She weighed only 35 kg when she returned to the Netherlands in 1945. She moved to Israel and became a nurse. She often visited schools to tell the story of her friend Anne Frank and of their meeting in Bergen-Belsen. Hannah found it a cruel twist of fate that she survived and Anne did not.

Sources

Anne Frank House –
Anne Frank House. A Museum with a Story,
translated by Lorraine T. Miller, 1999
Anne Frank House –
'Ik vond haar direct heel bijzonder ' ['I immediately thought she
was very special'], interview with Hello Silberberg,
Anne Frank Magazine, 1998
Anne Frank House / Annemarie de Leng –
'Ik wil over Anne vertellen' ['I would like to talk about Anne'],
interview with Hannah Pick-Goslar, Anne Frank Krant, 2015
Anne Frank Stichting (Eds.)
Anne Frank, Amsterdam: Keesing Boeken, 1979
Blitz Konig, Nanette
'Dat wij elkaar herkenden. Wij, twee skeletten' ['That we recognised
each other. Two skeletons'], article in *NRC Handelsblad,* 18 April 2016
Frank, Anne
Original diary manuscripts, versions A and B, 1942 - 1944
Frank, Anne
Letter, 13 January 1941
Frank, Anne
Letter, April 1942
Frank, Otto
Detailed models of two floors of the Annexe, article in *Het Vrije Volk,* 24
May 1962
Goldman Rubin, Susan
Searching for Anne Frank: Letters from Amsterdam to Iowa,
New York: Harry N. Abrahams, 2003
Kienzle, Birgit (Director)
Lasst mich so sein wie ich will. Anne Frank [Let me be myself. Anne
Frank], documentary, Südwestfunk, 1979
Maarsen, van, Jacqueline
*Je beste vriendin Anne. Herinneringen aan de oorlog en een
bijzondere vriendschap* [Your best friend Anne. Memories of the
war and a very special friendship], Amsterdam: Querido, 2011
Romein, Jan
Kinderstem [A child's voice], article in *Het Parool,* 3 April 1946
Roosevelt, Eleanor
Anne Frank: The Diary of a Young Girl, translated by B.M.
Mooyaart-Doubleday, New York: Doubleday & Company, Inc., 1952
Schnabel, Ernst
Footsteps of Anne Frank, translated by Richard and Clara Winston,
London: Southbank Publishing, 2015
Winter-Levy, de, Rosa
Aan de gaskamer ontsnapt! Het Satanswerk van de SS
[Escape from the gas chamber! The satanic work of the SS],
Doetinchem: Uitgevers-maatschappij "C. Misset", 1945
www.iisg.nl

Colophon

Published and produced by
Second Story Press
Copyright ©2018 Anne Frank
Stichting, Amsterdam
Text
Anne Frank House (Menno
Metselaar, Piet van Ledden)
Project management
Anne Frank House (Chantal
d´Aulnis)
Project coordination
Anne Frank House (Eugenie
Martens)
Historical research and super-
vision
Anne Frank House (Erika Prins,
Gertjan Broek)

Co-readers
Janny van der Molen
Waltraud Hüsmert
Anne Frank House (Femke de Koning)
Editing
Mieke Sobering
Final Edit
Vos l seo tekst & web (with Ingrid
Mersel)
final edit this edition: Kathryn Cole
and Natasha Bozorgi
Photo research
Anne Frank House (Karolien Stocking
Korzen)
Production support
Anne Frank House (Erica Terpstra)
this edition: Ellie Sipila
Design & typesetting
Joseph Plateau
Translation
NLtranslations.com

Library and Archives Canada Cataloguing in Publication
Metselaar, Menno
[Alles over Anne. English]
All about Anne / Menno Metselaar and Piet van Ledden ; Anne Frank's
life story, with answers to frequently asked questions and beautiful
drawings by Huck Scarry.

Translation of: Alles over Anne.
ISBN 978-1-77260-060-5 (hardcover)

1. Frank, Anne, 1929-1945--Juvenile literature. 2. Holocaust, Jewish
(1939-1945)--Netherlands--Amsterdam--Juvenile literature. 3. Jews--
Persecutions--Netherlands--Amsterdam--Juvenile literature. 4. Nether-
lands--
History--German occupation, 1940-1945--Juvenile literature. I. Ledden, Piet
van, author II. Scarry, Huck, illustrator III. Anne Frank House, creator
IV. Title. V. Title: Alles over Anne. English.

DS135.N6F73494313 2018   j940.53'18092   C2018-901705-8

Printed in China

*Second Story Press gratefully acknowledges the support of the
Ontario Arts Council and the Canada Council for the Arts for our
publishing program. We acknowledge the financial support of the
Government of Canada through the Canada Book Fund*

ONTARIO ARTS COUNCIL
CONSEIL DES ARTS DE L'ONTARIO

Canada Council   Conseil des Arts
for the Arts   du Canada

Funded by the Government of Canada
Financé par le gouvernement du Canada

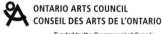

Canada

Everything about Anne in one book?
Of course that's not possible.

Hopefully you even have some new questions.
You can often find answers on our website www.annefrank.org,
or in other books written about Anne Frank.
You can also read 'Anne Frank. *The diary of a young girl.*',
the most famous publication of Anne's diaries!
If you cannot find the answer to your question anywhere,
please let us know: mijnvraag@annefrank.nl